HOW TO DRAW "ALMOST" EVERYTHING FOR KIDS

300 CUTE STEP-BY-STEP DRAWINGS OF ANIMALS, INSECTS, DINOSAURS, SPACE, FAST FOOD AND OTHER AMAZING STUFF!

This belongs to :

....

Special Art Learning

"How to Draw 'Almost' Everything for Kids"

300 Cute Step-by-Step Drawings of Animals, Insects, Dinosaurs, Space, Fast Food and Other Amazing Stuff!

© 2024 by Special Art

All rights reserved. No part of this publication may be reproduced, distributed, or transmitted in any form or by any means, including photocopying, recording, or other electronic or mechanical methods, without the prior written permission of the publisher, except for brief quotations in reviews or non-commercial uses permitted by copyright law. For permissions, contact: support@specialartbooks.com.

Published by Special Art Books
www.specialartbooks.com

Paperback ISBN:
Images © Shutterstock

Table of Contents

Animals and Insects

AARDVARK 3
ALBATROSS 3
ALLIGATOR 3
ALPACA 4
ANGELFISH 4
ANT 4
ANT (BACK) 5
ANTELOPE 5
APE 5
ARCTIC FOX 6
ARMADILLO 6
AXOLOTL 6
BABOON 7
BAT 7
BEAR 7
BEAR (SITTING) 8
BEAVER 8
BEE 8
BEE (FUNNY) 9
BEETLE 9

BIRD 9
BISON 10
BUFFALO 10
BUFFALO (READING A BOOK) 10
BULL 11
BUNNY 11
BUNNY WITH CARROT 11
BUNNY WITH STRAWBERRIES 12
BURRO 12
BUTTERFLY 12
CARDINAL 13
CAT 13
CATFISH 13
CATERPILLAR 14
CENTIPEDE 14
CHAMELEON 14
CHICKEN 15
CHICKEN (EDGY) 15

CHIMPANZEE 15
CICADA 16
CLOWNFISH 16
COBRA 16
COCKROACH 17
COW 17
COYOTE 17
CRAB 18
CRICKET 18
CROCODILE 18
CROW 19
DACHSHUND 19
DEER 19
DINGO 20
DISCUS 20
DODO 20
DOG 21
DOLPHIN 21
DONKEY 21
DRAGONFLY 22

DUCK 22	JELLYFISH 31	SEA OTTER 40
DUGONG 22	KID 31	SEAGULL 40
EAGLE 23	KOALA 32	SEAHORSE 41
EARTHWORM 23	LADYBUG 32	SHARK 41
ECHIDNA 23	LION 32	SHEEP 41
EEL 24	LION (SLEEPING) 33	SHRIMP 42
EGRET 24	LIZARD 33	SKUNK 42
ELEPHANT 24	MACAW 33	SLOTH 42
EMU 25	MONKEY 34	SNAIL 43
ERMINE 25	MOSQUITO 34	SNAIL (FUNNY) 43
FIREFLY 25	MOUSE 34	SPIDER 43
FISH 26	OCTOPUS 35	SPIDER (SLEEPY) 44
FLAMINGO 26	OWL 35	SQUID 44
FLY 26	PANDA 35	SQUIRREL 44
FOX 27	PARROT 36	STARFISH 45
FROG 27	PEACOCK 36	STINGRAY 45
GIRAFFE 27	PELICAN 36	TIGER 45
GOAT 28	PENGUIN 37	TOUCAN 46
GOOSE 28	PIG 37	TURKEY 46
GRASSHOPPER 28	PIGEON 37	TURTLE 46
HEDGEHOG 29	PLATYPUS 38	WALRUS 47
HIPPOPOTAMUS 29	PORCUPINE 38	WARBLER 47
HONEYBEE 29	PUFFERFISH 38	WHALE 47
HORNBILL 30	PUG 39	WORM 48
HORSE 30	RACCOON 39	ZEBRA 48
HUMMINGBIRD 30	REINDEER 39	
IGUANA 31	RHINO 40	

Vehicles and Machines

AIRCRAFT 50	DINGHY 54	MOTORCYCLE 58
AIRPLANE 50	DUMP TRUCK 54	POLICE CAR 58
AMBULANCE 50	EXCAVATOR 54	ROWBOAT 58
ARMY TANK 51	F1 RACING CAR 55	SAILBOAT 59
BICYCLE 51	FORKLIFT 55	SPEED TRAIN 59
BOAT 51	FUEL TANKER 55	SUBMARINE 59
BULLDOZER 52	GLIDER 56	TRACTOR 60
BUS 52	HELICOPTER 56	TRAIN 60
CAMPER VAN 52	HOT AIR BALLOON 56	TRUCK 60
CAR 53	JET 57	VAN 61
CARGO TRUCK 53	LIMOUSINE 57	YACHT 61
COMPACT CAR 53	LOCOMOTIVE 57	

Dinosaurs, Ghosts and Monsters

AMARGASAURUS 63
BRACHIOSAURUS 63
CANDY CORN MONSTER 63
DINO ORIGAMI 64
EYEBALL BOTTLE 64
FAT DINOSAUR 64
HALLOWEEN BLACK CAT 65
HALLOWEEN BLACK GHOST 65
HALLOWEEN GHOST 65
HAPPY GHOST 66

JACK-O'-LANTERN 66
MONSTER 66
MUMMY 67
PARASAUROLOPHUS 67
PIRATE GHOST 67
PSITTACOSAURUS 68
PTERODACTYL 68
PUMPKIN DEMON 68
PUMPKIN GIRL 69
PUMPKIN SKELETON 69
SILLY DINOSAUR 69

SKELETON GHOST 70
SPINOSAURUS 70
STEGOSAURUS 70
T-REX 71
TRICK OR TREAT GHOST 71
VOODOO DOLL GHOST 71
WEREWOLF 72
WEREWOLF GHOST 72
WITCH GHOST 72
ZOMBIE GHOST 73

Space and Sci-Fi

ALIEN 75
ASTEROID 75
ASTRONAUT WITH FLAG 75
COMET 76
LAB FLASK 76
LUNAR ROVER 76
MAGNET 77

MICROSCOPE 77
RAY GUN 77
ROBOT (SMILING) 78
ROBOT WITH ROUND HEAD 78
ROBOT 78
ROCKET 79

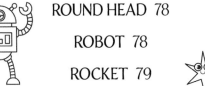

SATELLITE (SMILING) 79
SATELLITE 79
SHOOTING STAR 80
SPACE ROCKET LAUNCH 80
SUN 80
TELESCOPE 81
UFO 81

Sports, Fast Food and Everyday Things

ALARM CLOCK 83
BABY 83
BAG 83
BASKETBALL 84
BED 84
BOOKCASE 84
BOTTLE OF COLA 85
BOTTLE OF LEMONADE 85
BOTTLE OF ORANGE JUICE 85
BOTTLE OF SODA 86
BOTTLE OF STRAWBERRY JUICE 86
BOWL OF RAMEN 86
CACTUS 87
CAMERA 87
CEMENT TRUCK 87
CHAIR 88
CHILI SAUCE 88
COINS 88
COMPASS 89
COMPUTER SETUP 89
COTTAGE 89
CUP NOODLES WITH CHOPSTICKS 90
CUP NOODLES 90
DRUM 90
EYEGLASSES 91

FEATHER 91
FISHBONE 91
FLOWERS 92
FOOTBALL, SOCCER, AND BASKETBALL 92
FOOTBALL 92
FRIES 93
GLASS OF LEMONADE 93
GUITAR 93
HAMBURGER 94
HAMMER 94
HEADPHONES 94
HEELS 95
HOT DOG 95
INSTANT NOODLES 95
IRON 96
KETCHUP 96
KEY 96
LAMP 97
LAPTOP 97
LEATHER SHOES 97
LUGGAGE 98
MOBILE PHONE 98
MUSHROOMS 98
NOODLES IN A BOX 99
ONIGIRI 99
PIZZA 99

PLIERS 100
RAINBOOTS 100
SAFETY GOGGLES 100
SANDWICH 101
SAUSAGES 101
SCISSORS 101
SLIPPERS 102
SNEAKERS 102
SOCCER 102
SUITCASE 103
SURFBOARD 103
TABLE 103
TACO 104
TEACUP 104
TELEPHONE 104
TOASTER 105
TRASH CAN 105
TV 105
UMBRELLA 106
VACUUM 106
VIOLIN 106
WASHING MACHINE 107
WATCH 107
WHEAT 107
WOODEN CHAIR 108
XYLOPHONE 108

INTRODUCTION

Welcome to the world of drawing! Whether you want to draw dinosaurs, cool vehicles, or even aliens, this book will guide you on how to start drawing. How can a couple of circles and lines end up looking like a space rocket? Here's a secret: drawing anything starts with the simplest shapes, so you definitely can do it!

This book is packed with tips and tricks to help you draw like a pro. So grab your pencils and unleash your creativity. With a few practice sketches and your awesome imagination, you'll become the artist you've always wanted to be! And soon you'll learn to draw almost everything!

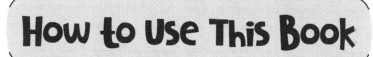

How to Use This Book

You don't need a lot of tools when you practice drawing. You can use your favorite pencil and some of the crayons that you already have. Mistakes can happen, so remember to keep an eraser close by too! If you want to add some color to your artwork, consider these additional supplies:

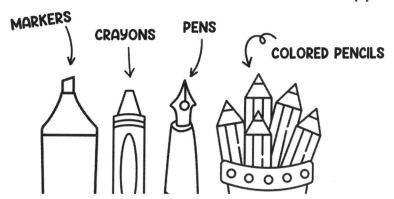

When sketching with your pencil, draw gently to keep your lines clean and make corrections easy. Lightly trace and follow the arrows to complete your drawing. Afterwards, there's space for you to practice drawing on each activity page. Use the pages of this book as your drawing space and fill it up with your art—yes, you can even draw on the margins!

So what are you waiting for? Start drawing and have fun!

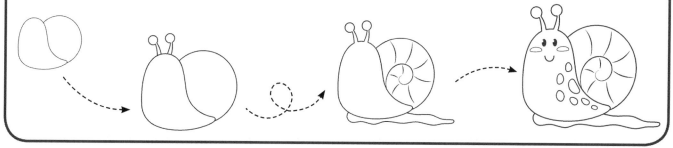

Animals and Insects

Animals are some of the cutest creatures in this world. What's your favorite animal? In this chapter, you'll learn to draw animals and insects, from the tiniest ant to the giant whale! Let's begin!

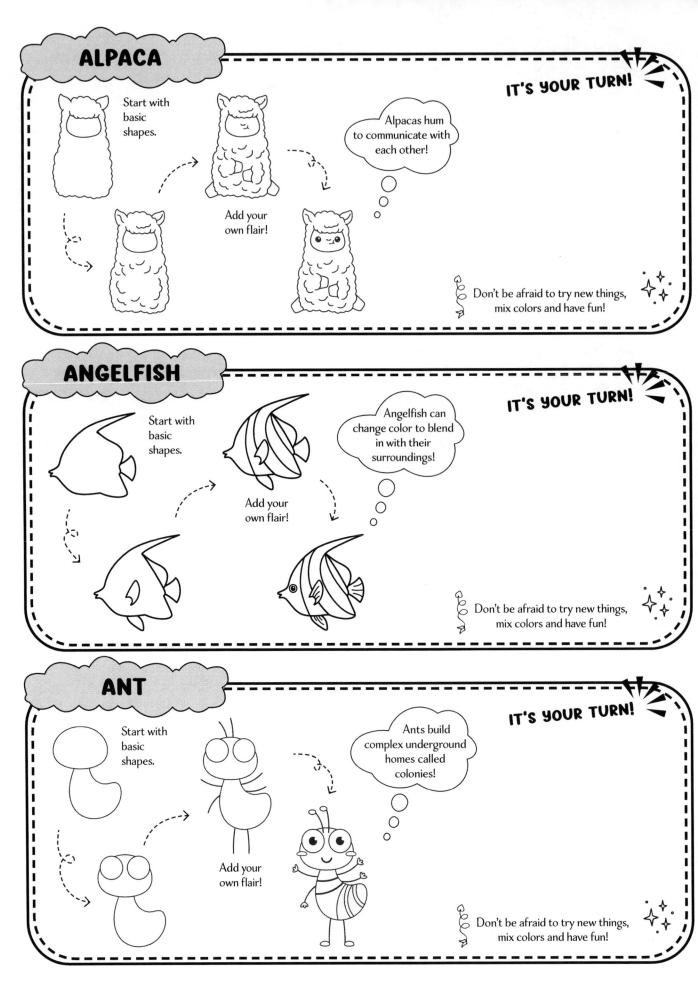

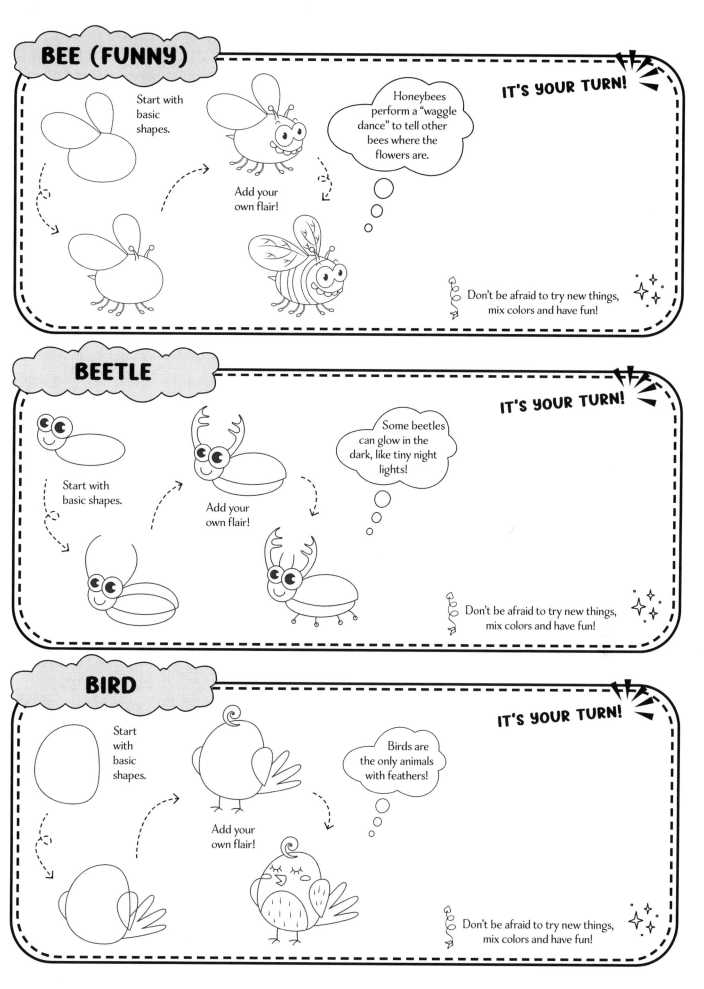

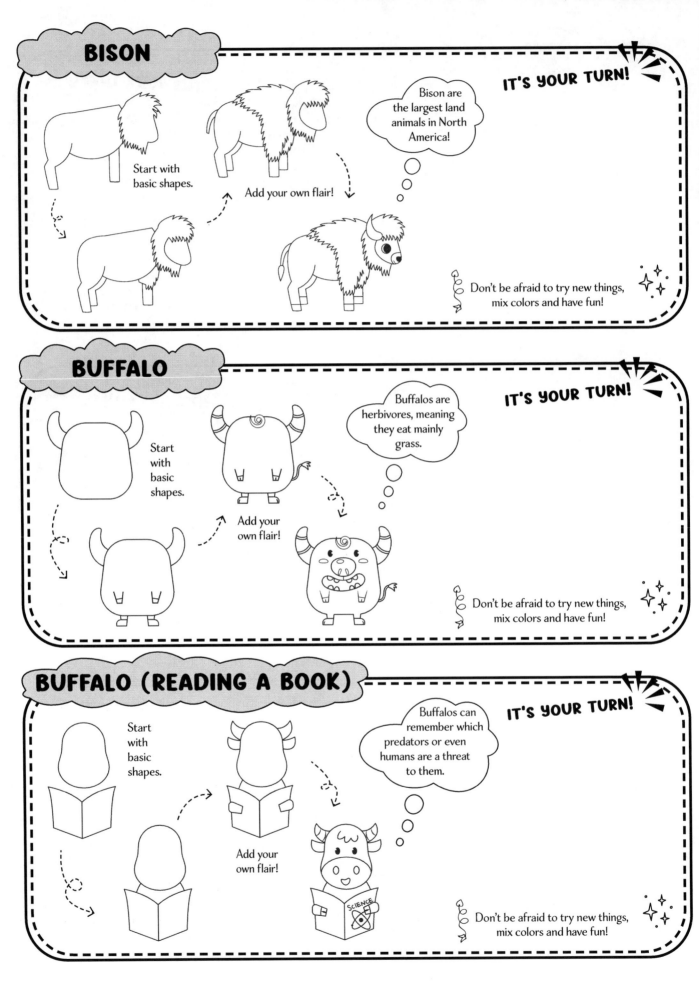

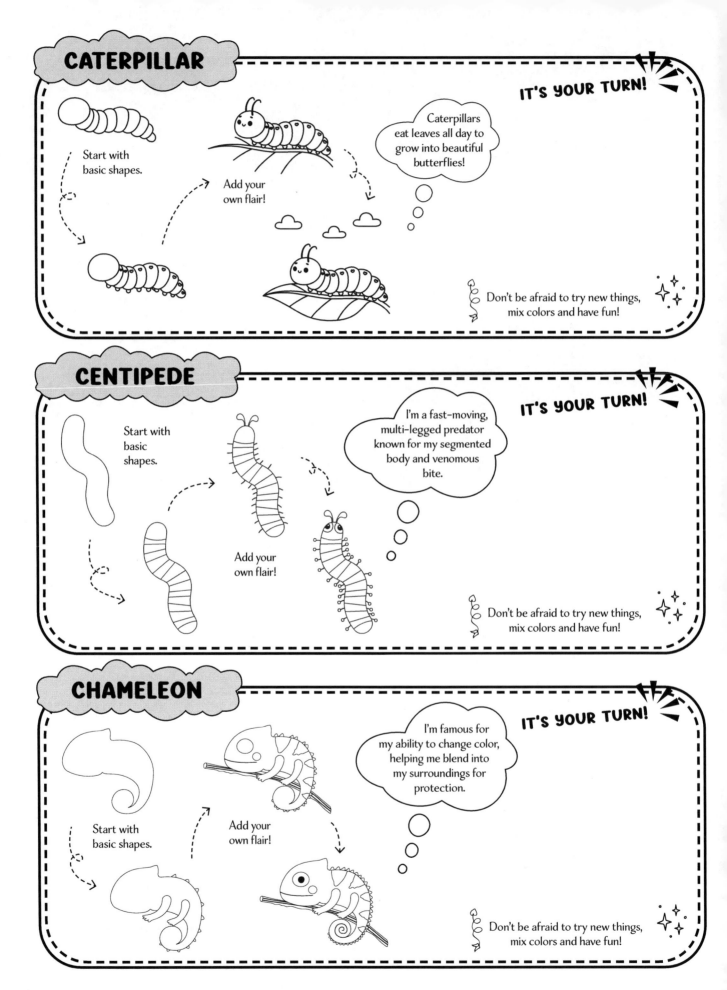

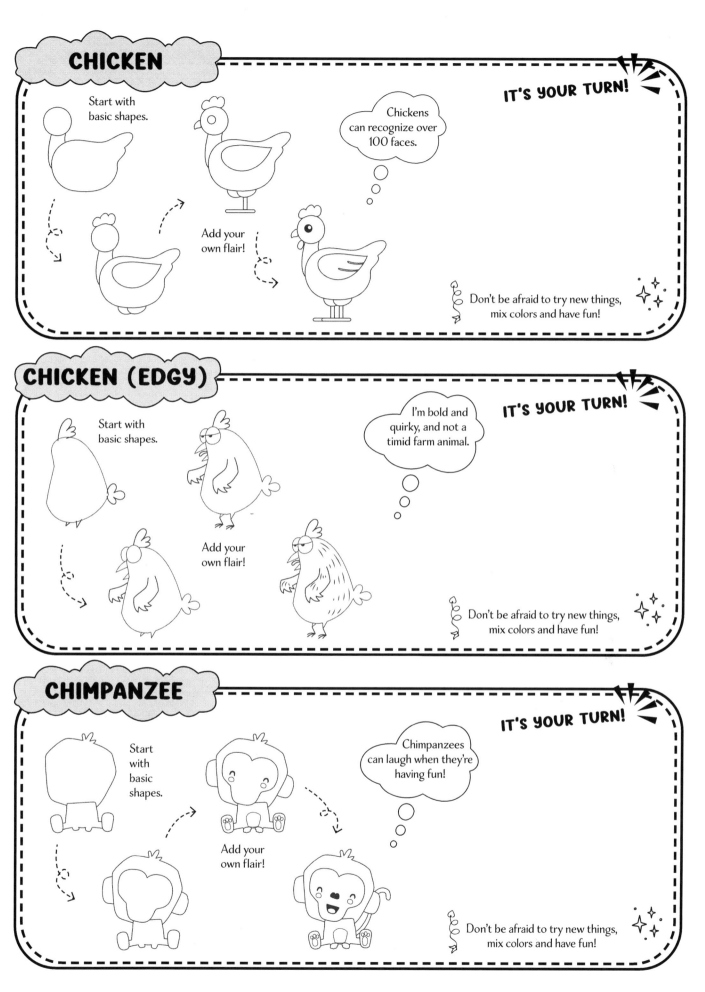

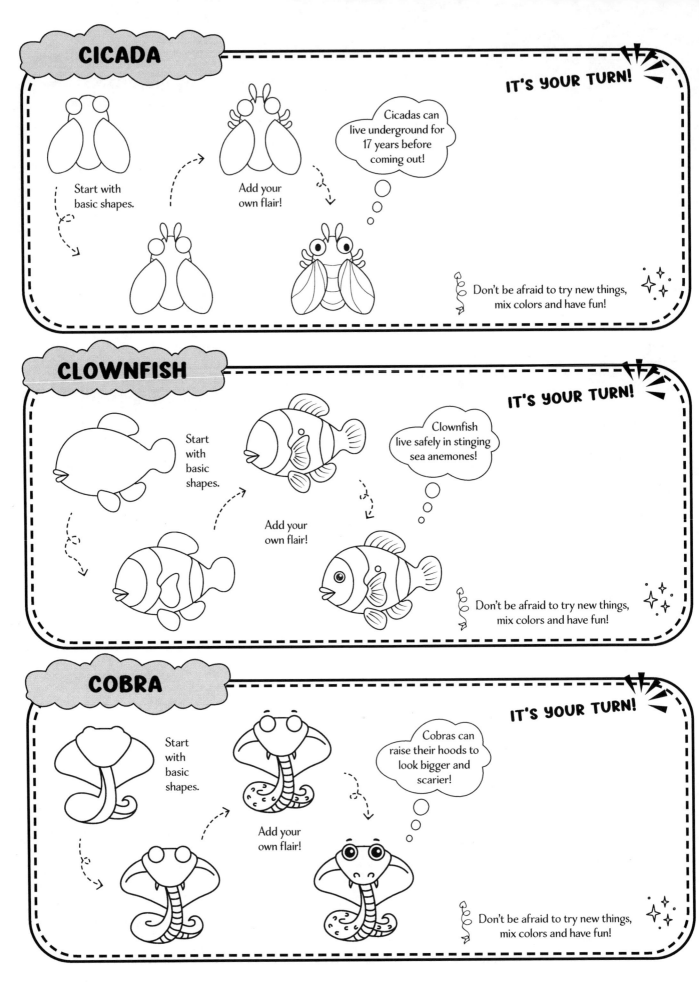

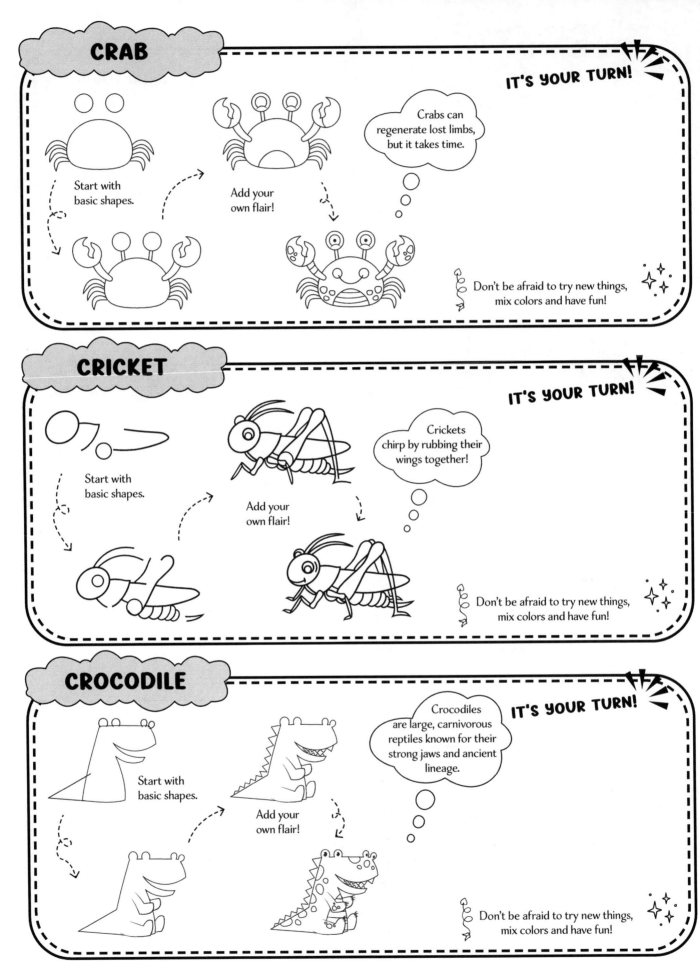

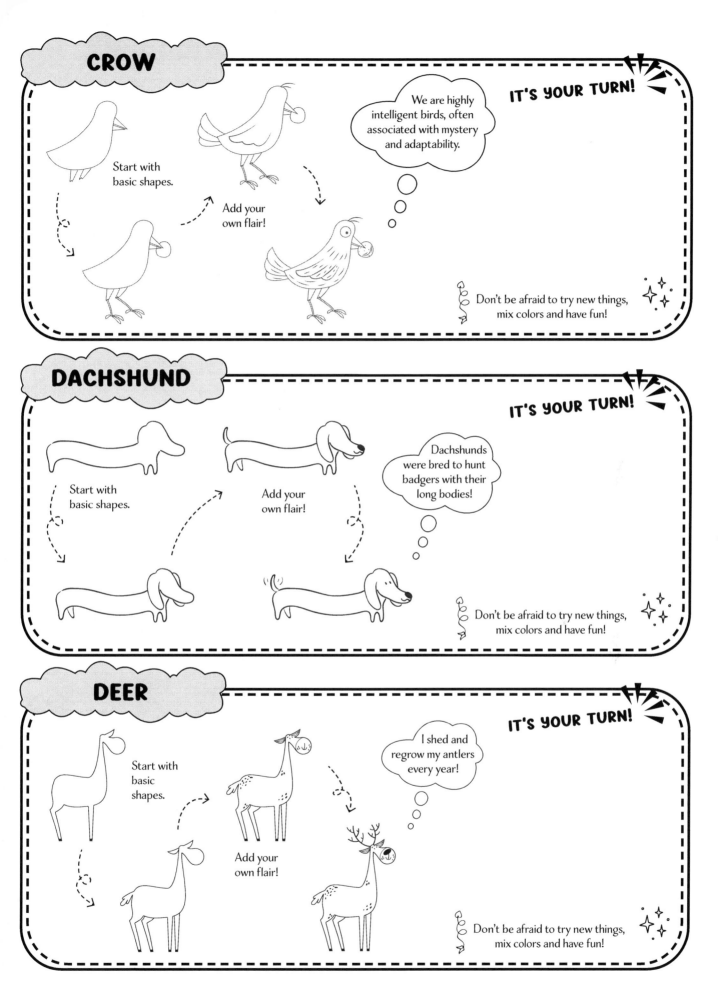

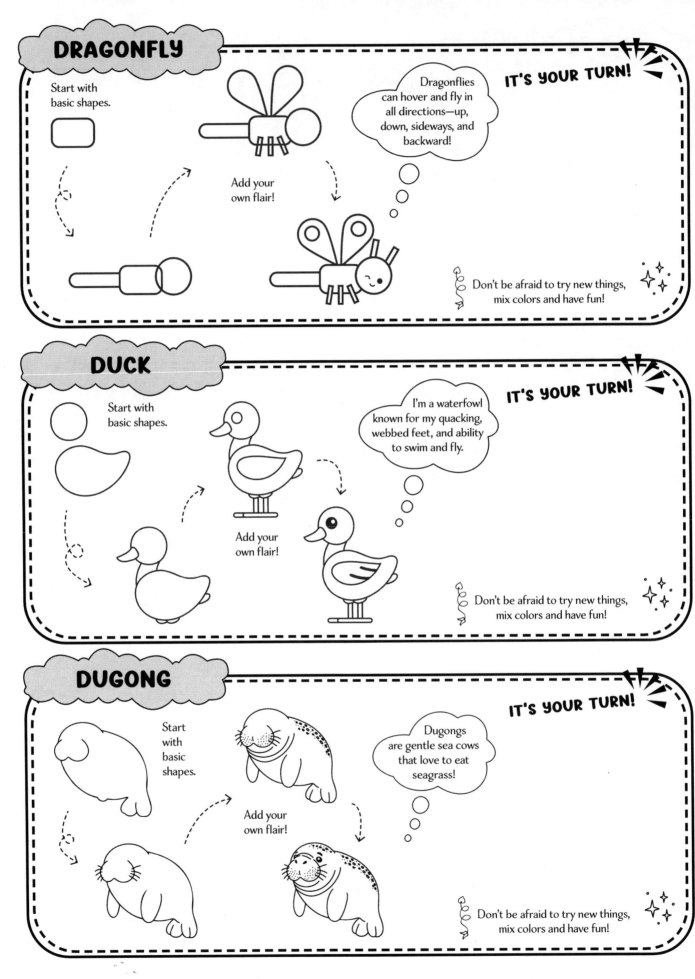

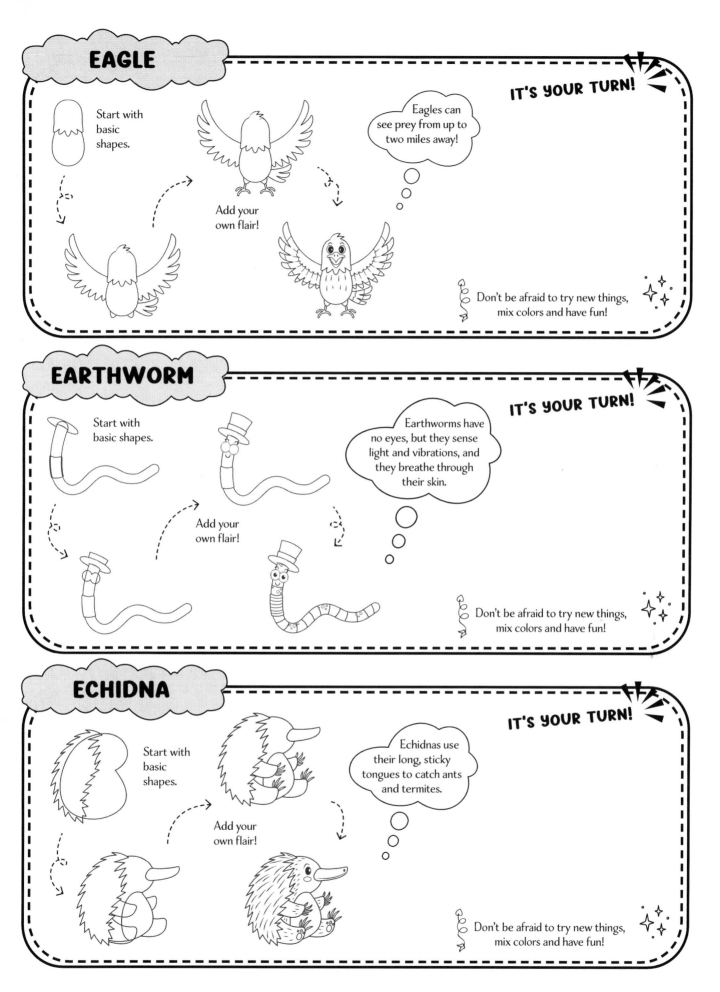

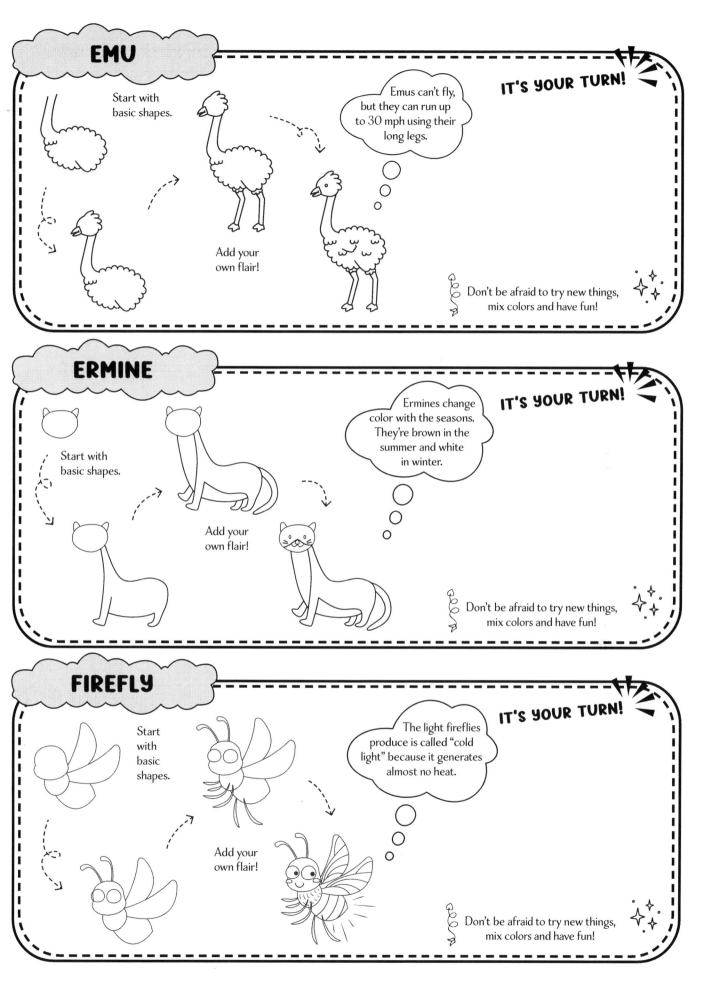

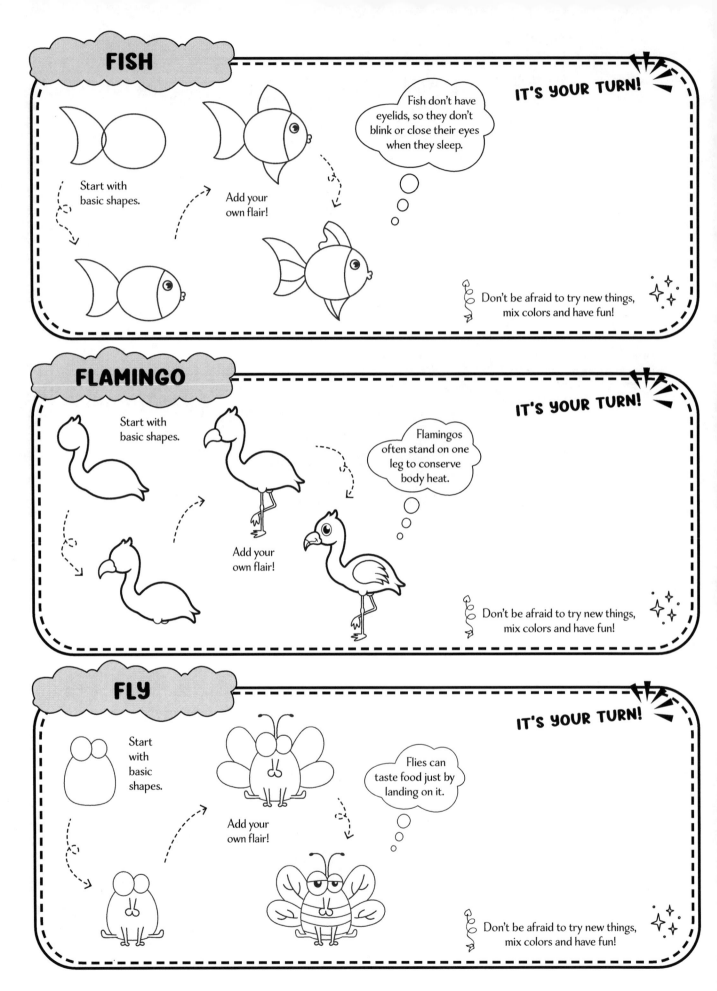

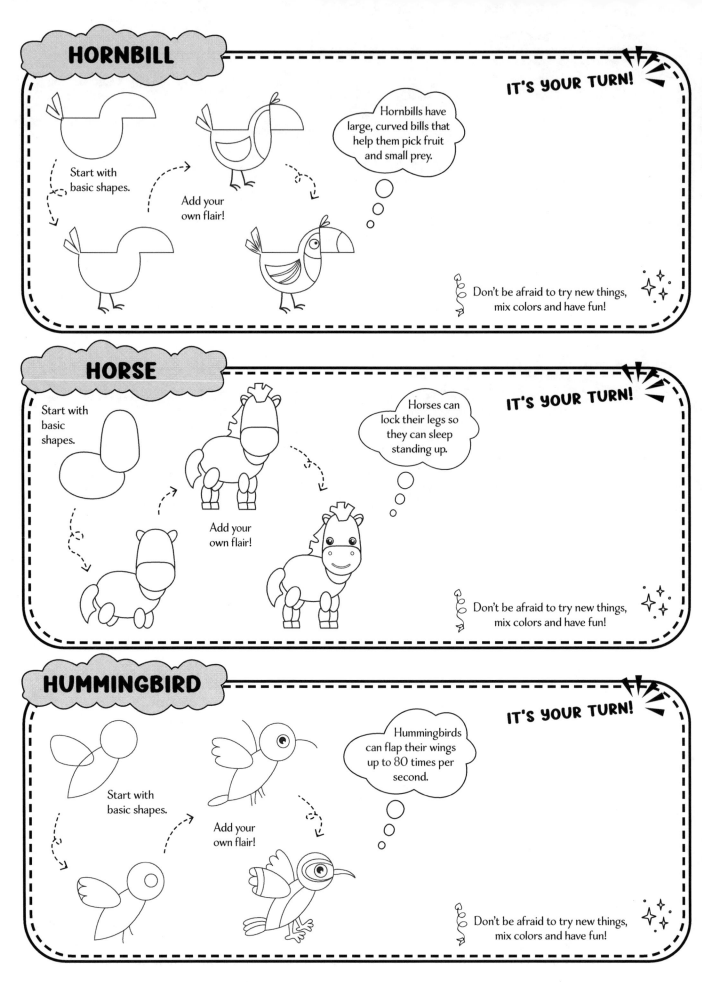

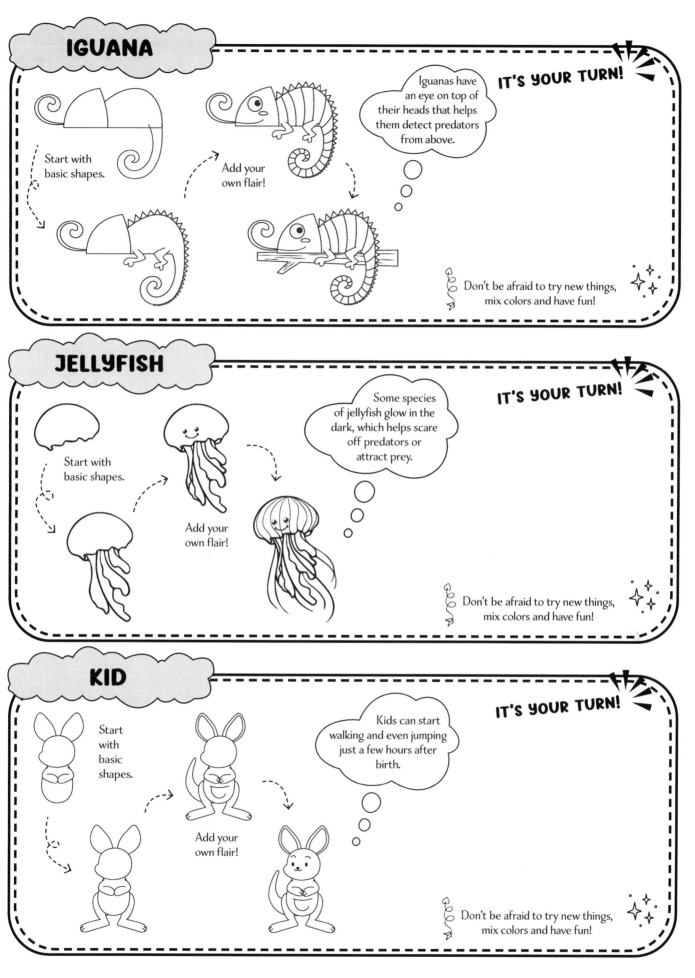

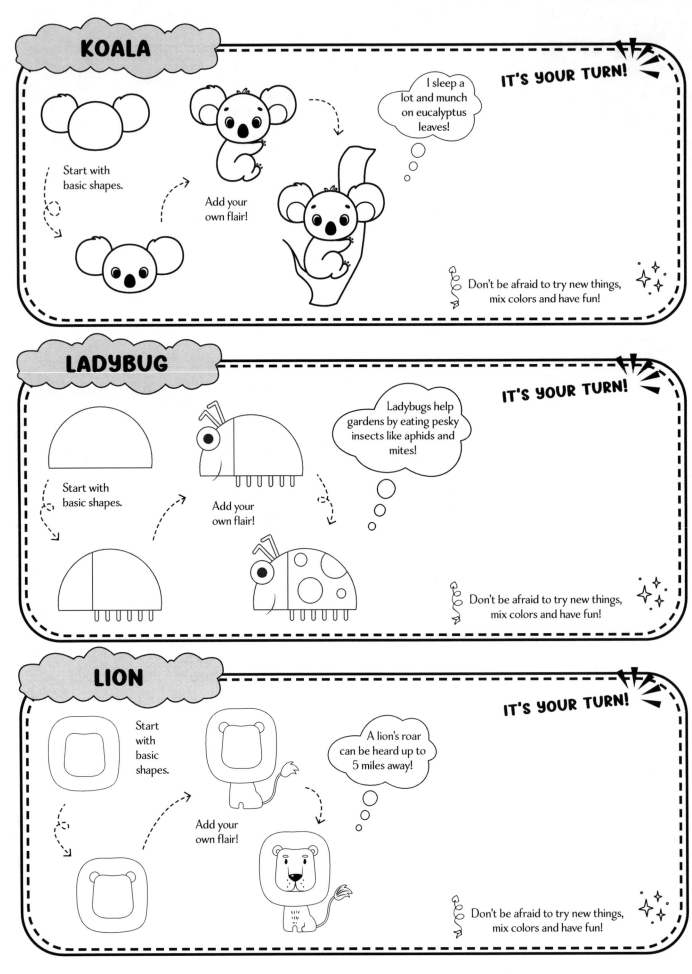

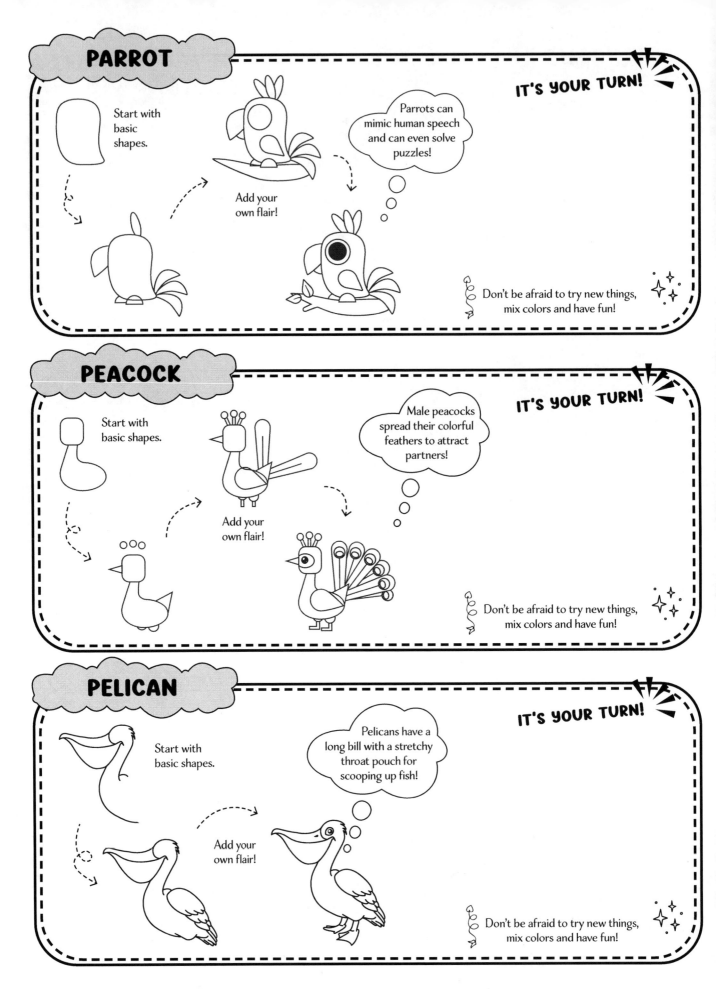

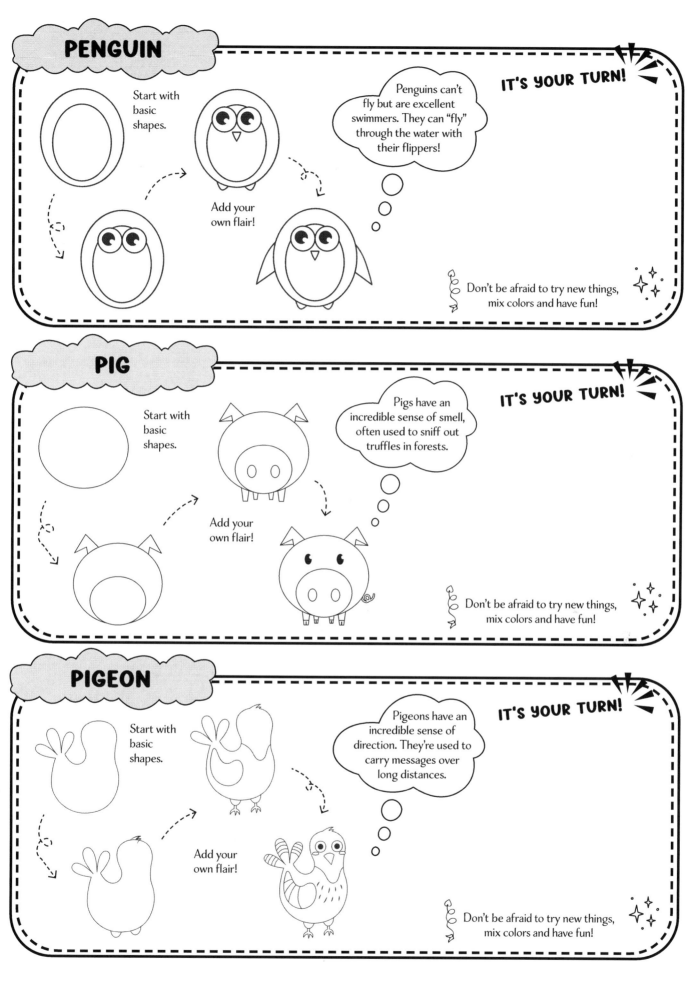

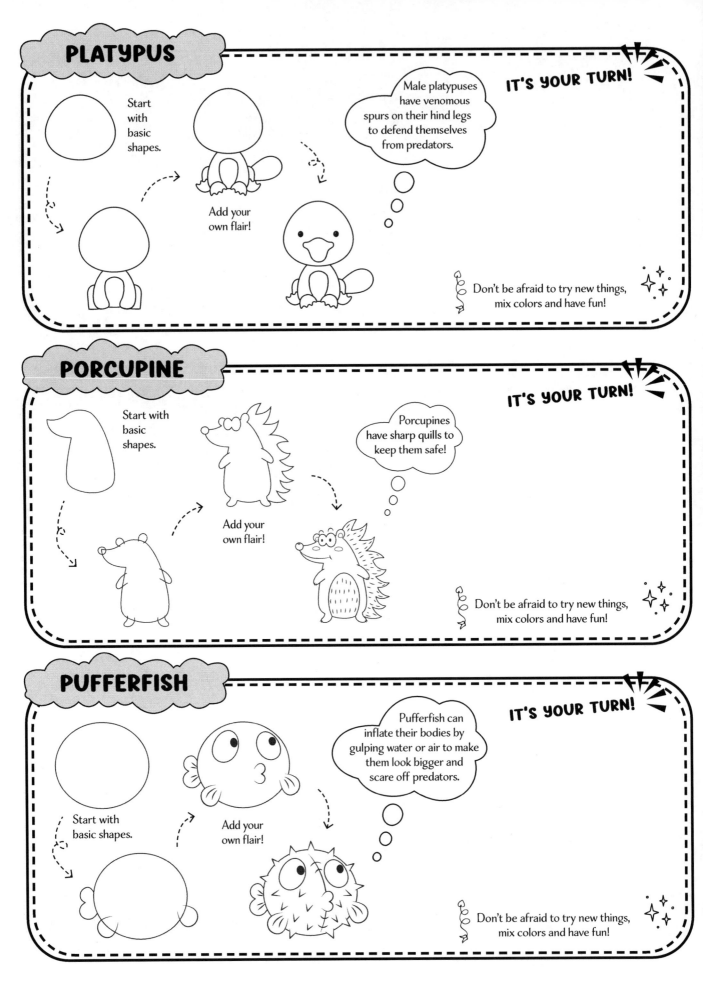

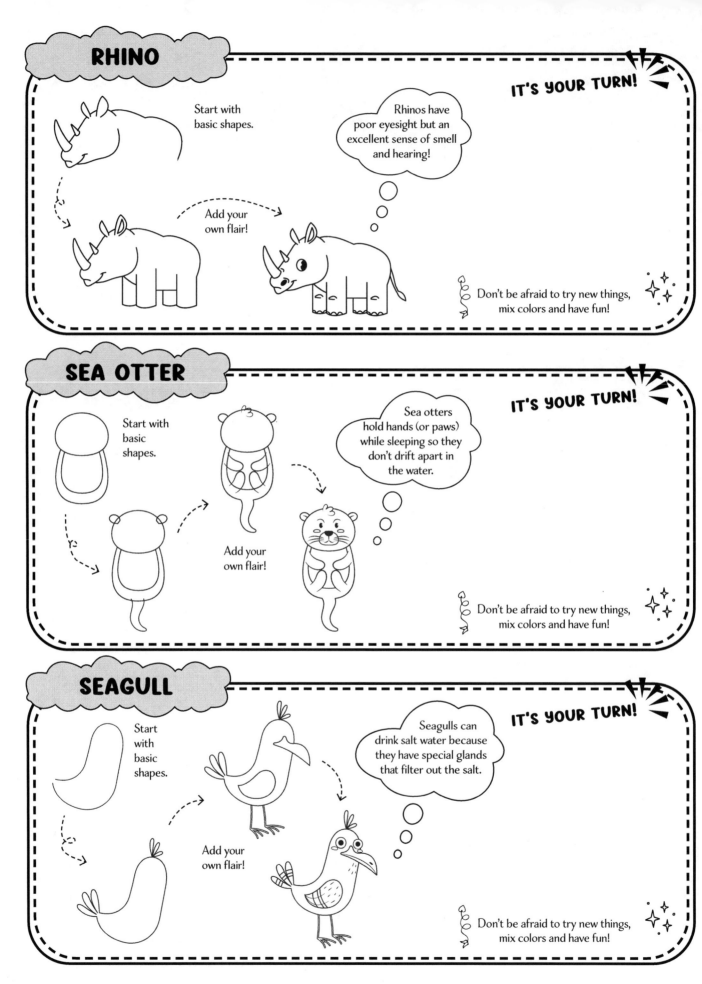

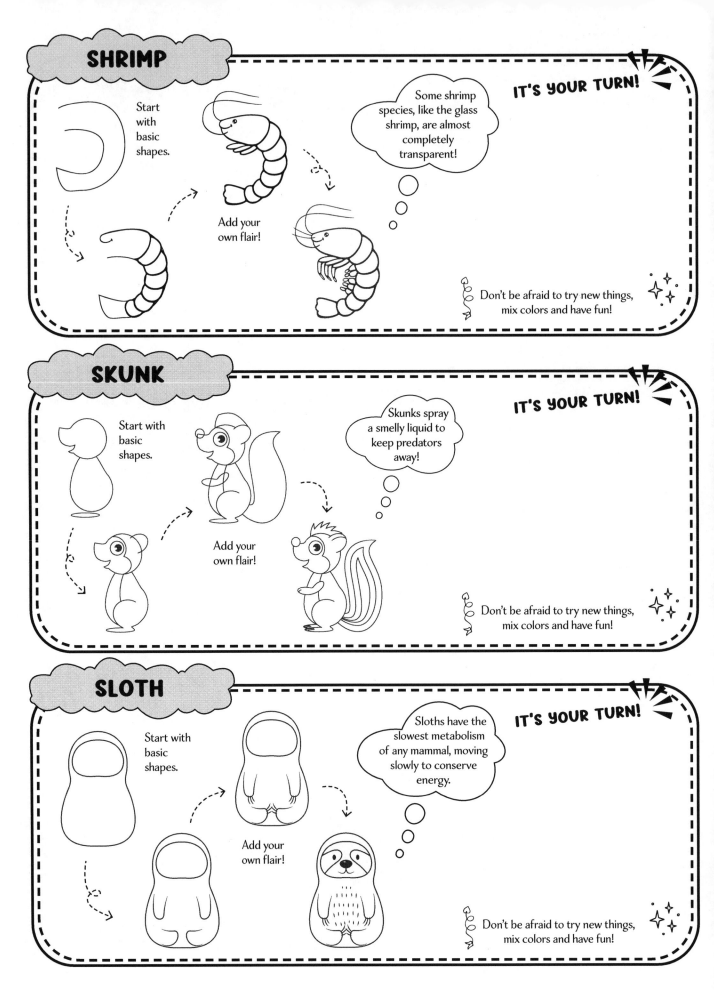

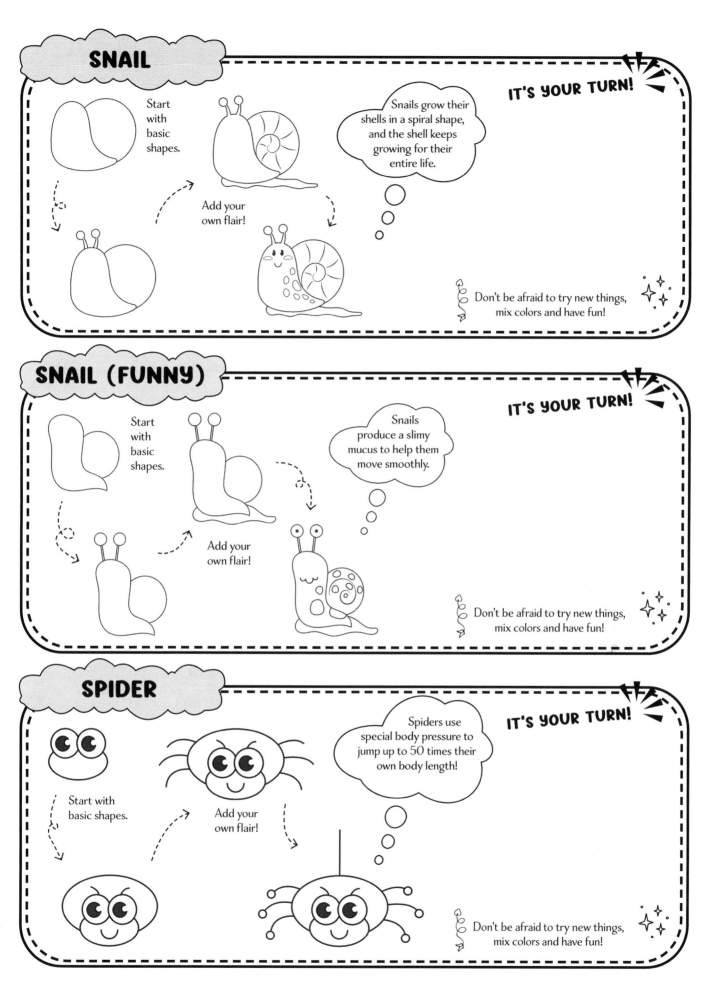

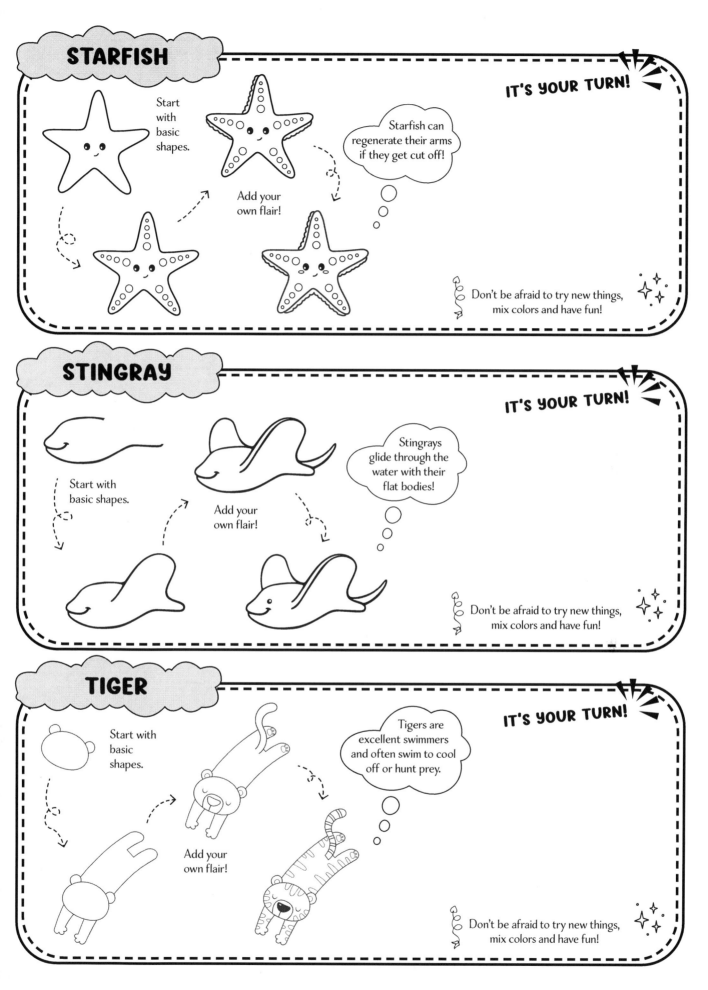

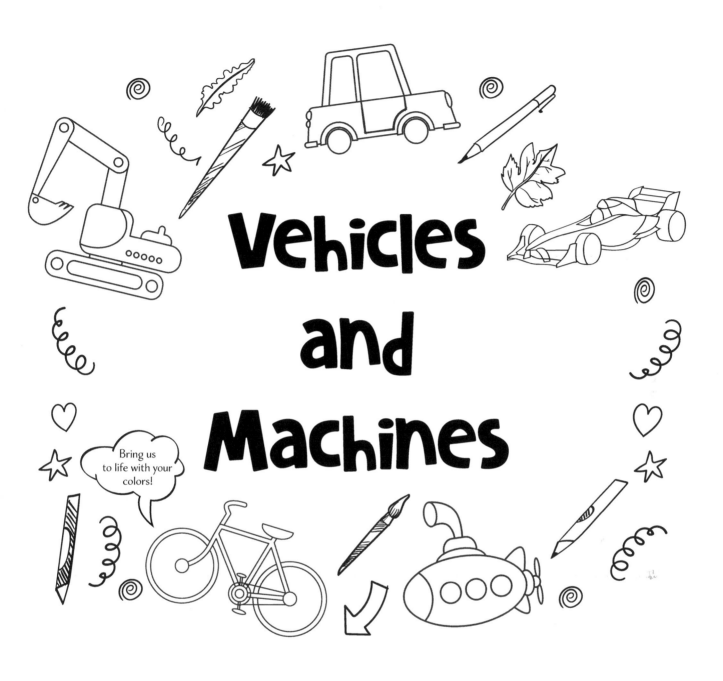

Vehicles and Machines

Did you know that most **machines** and **vehicles** have some kind of wheel? Even **boats** have **wheels steering wheels**! In this chapter, you'll start drawing **gliders, buses, excavators**, and other **cool vehicles**!

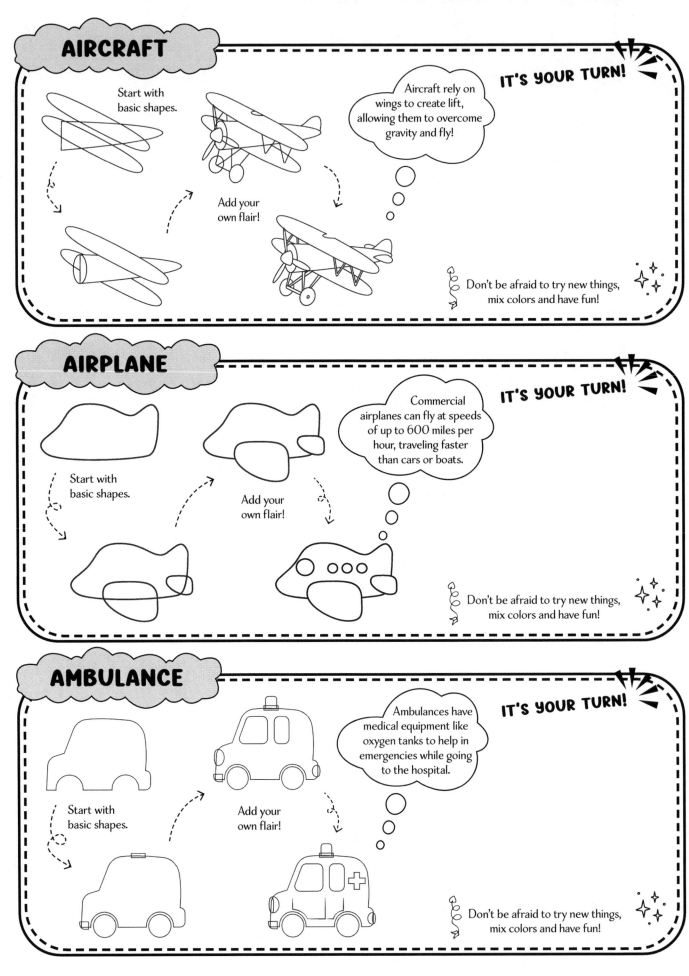

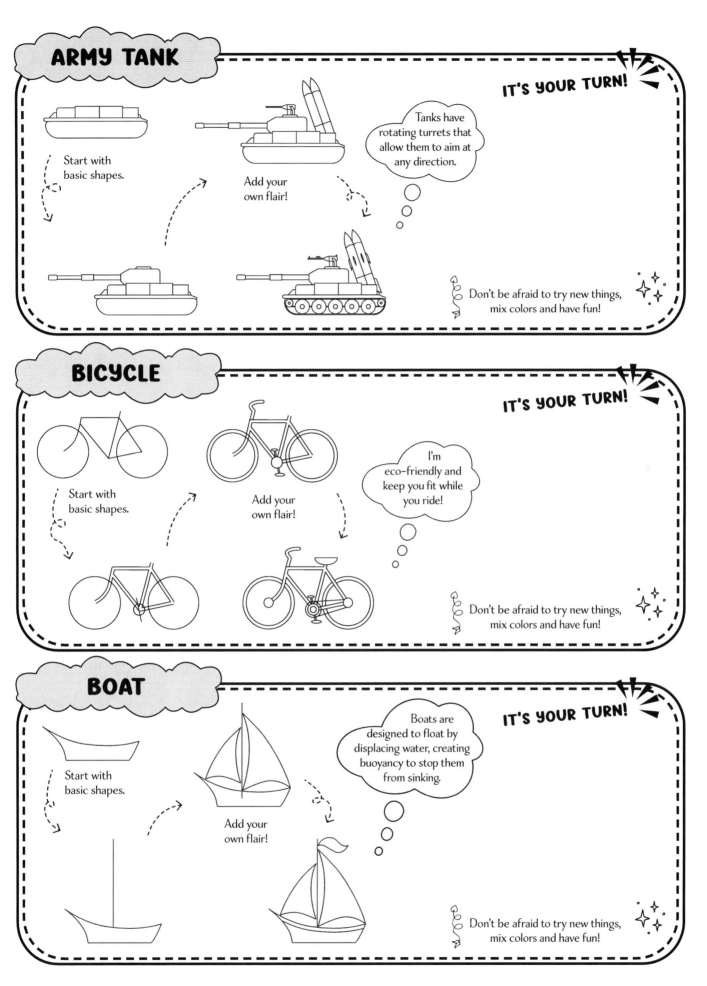

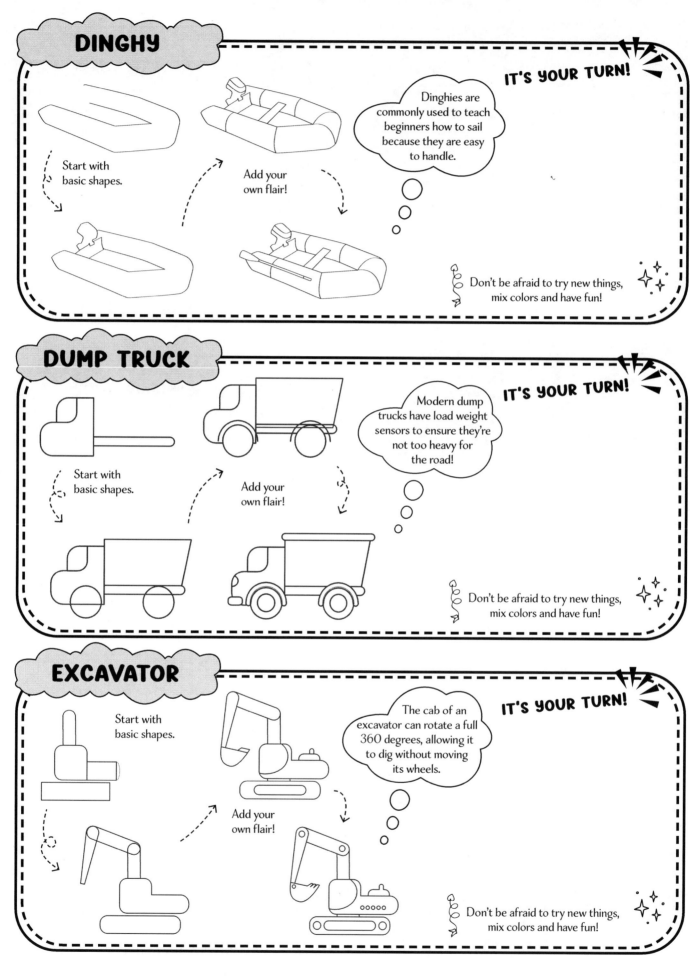

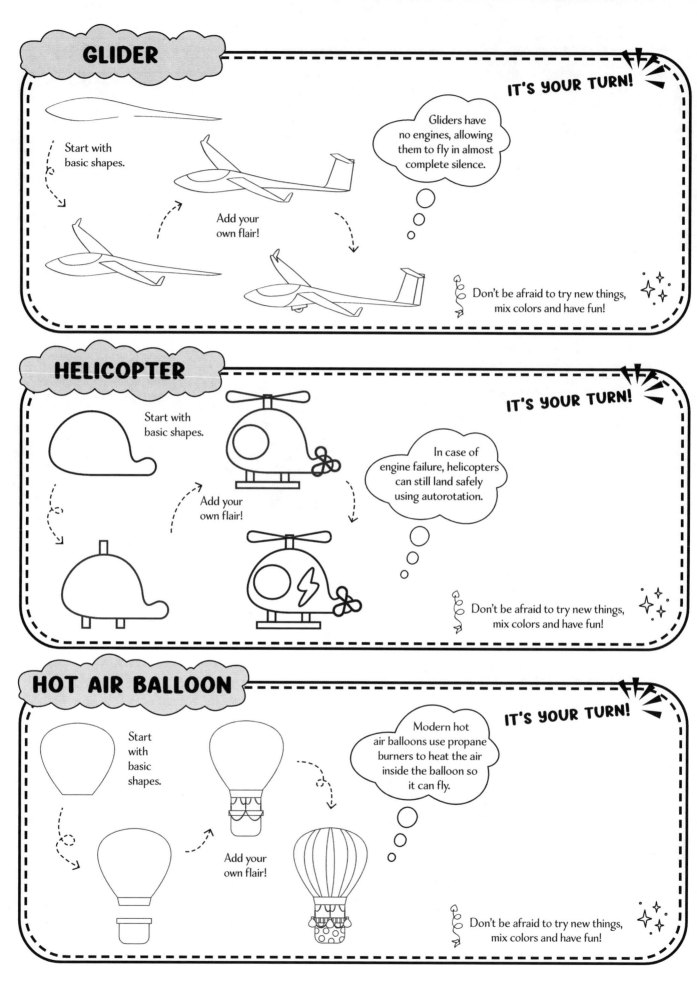

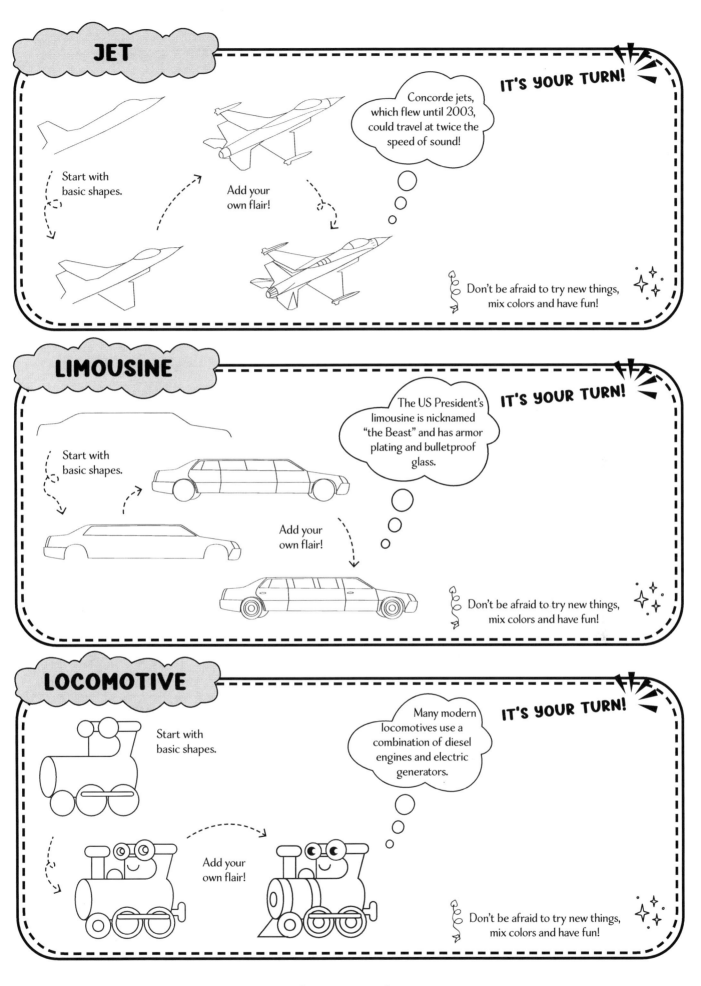

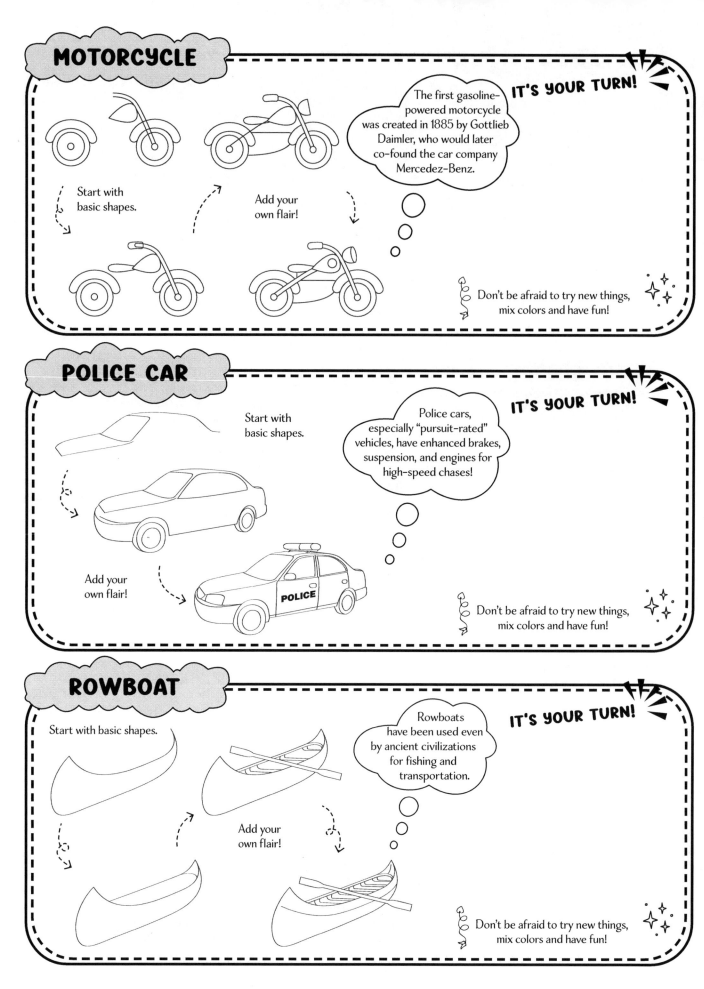

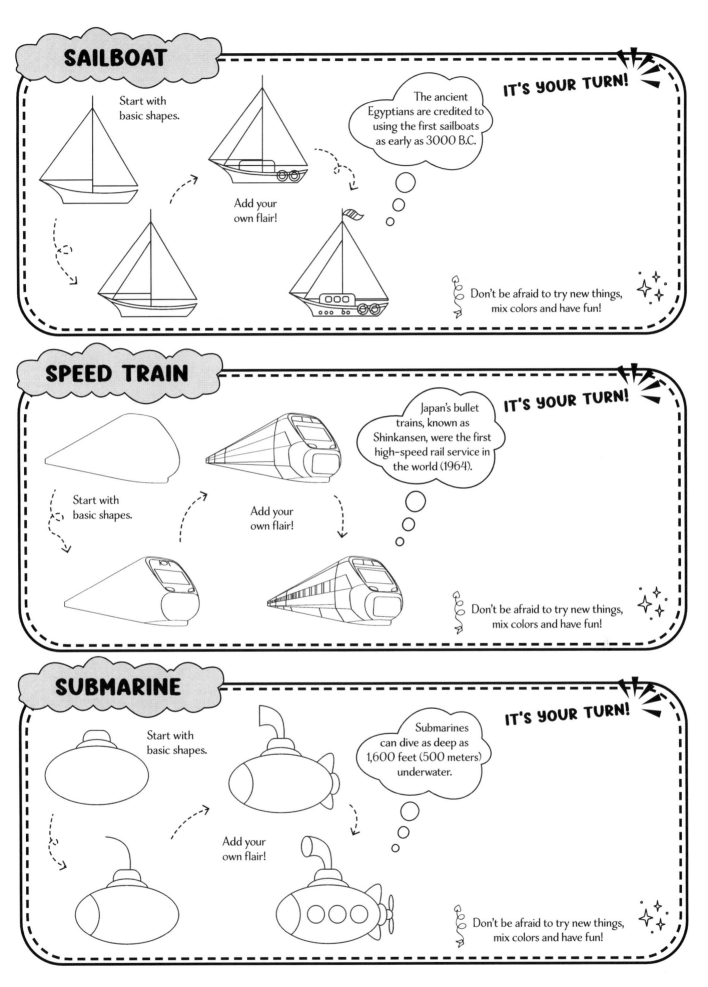

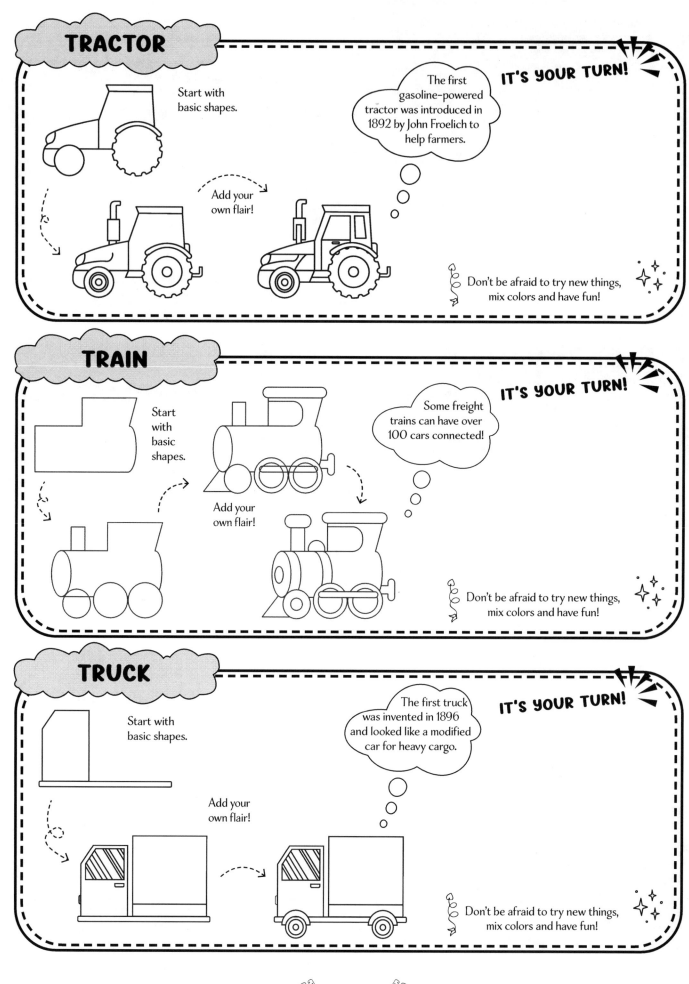

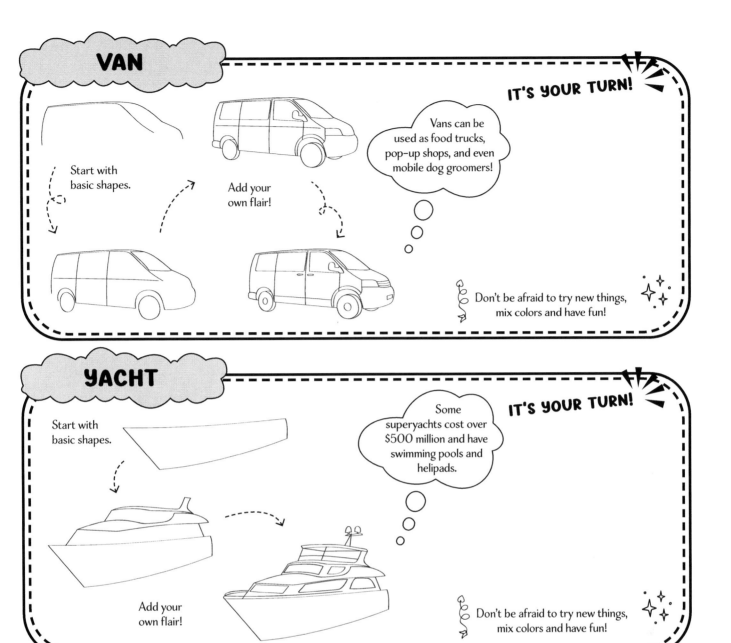

Dinosaurs, Ghosts and Monsters

Bring us to life with your colors!

Do you like drawing **dinosaurs**?
What about **Jack-o'-lanterns**?
In this chapter, you'll start to draw some common **dinosaurs**, **spooky ghosts**, and even **pumpkins**!
Let's begin!

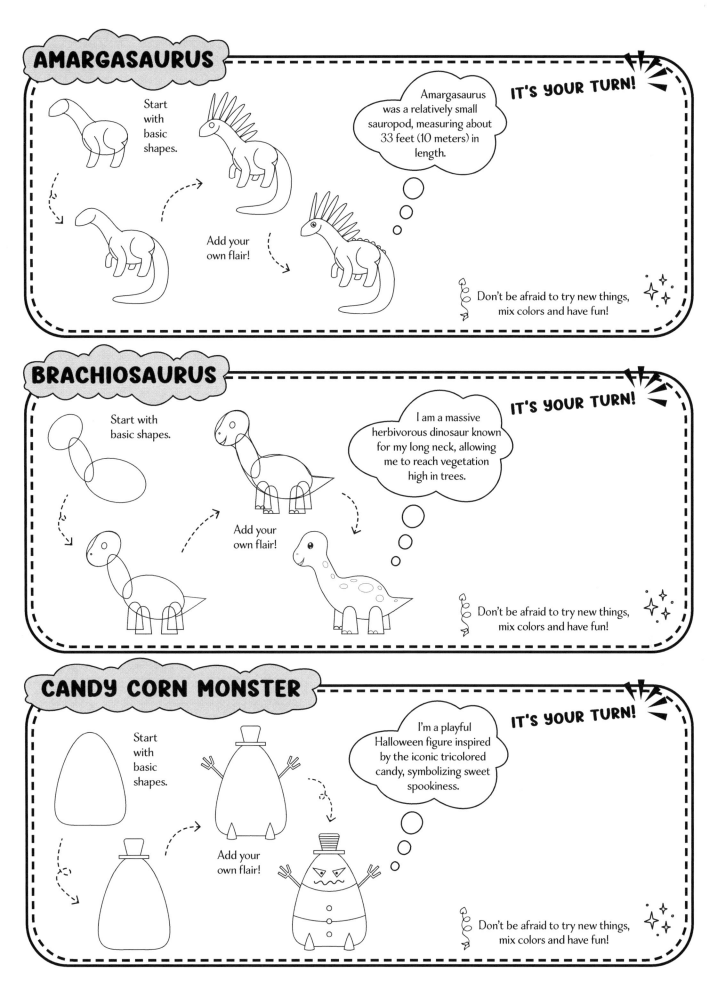

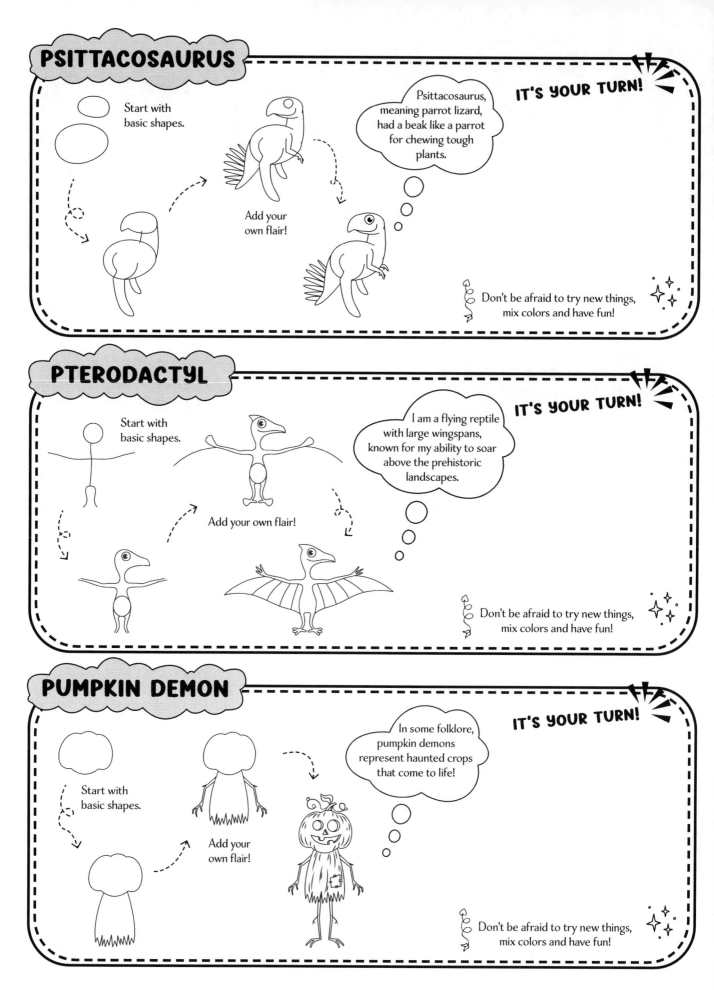

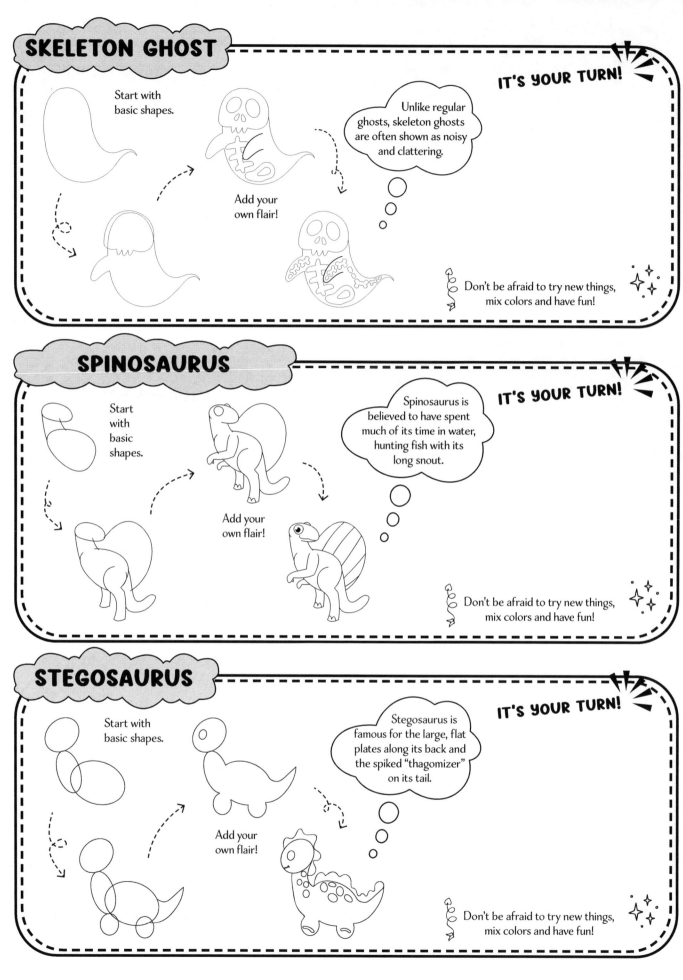

Space and Sci-Fi

Bring us to life with your colors!

Have you ever seen a **space rocket** launch into the sky? They're really cool, right? Let's learn to draw some **space technology** and **science** items, even **robots** and **aliens**!

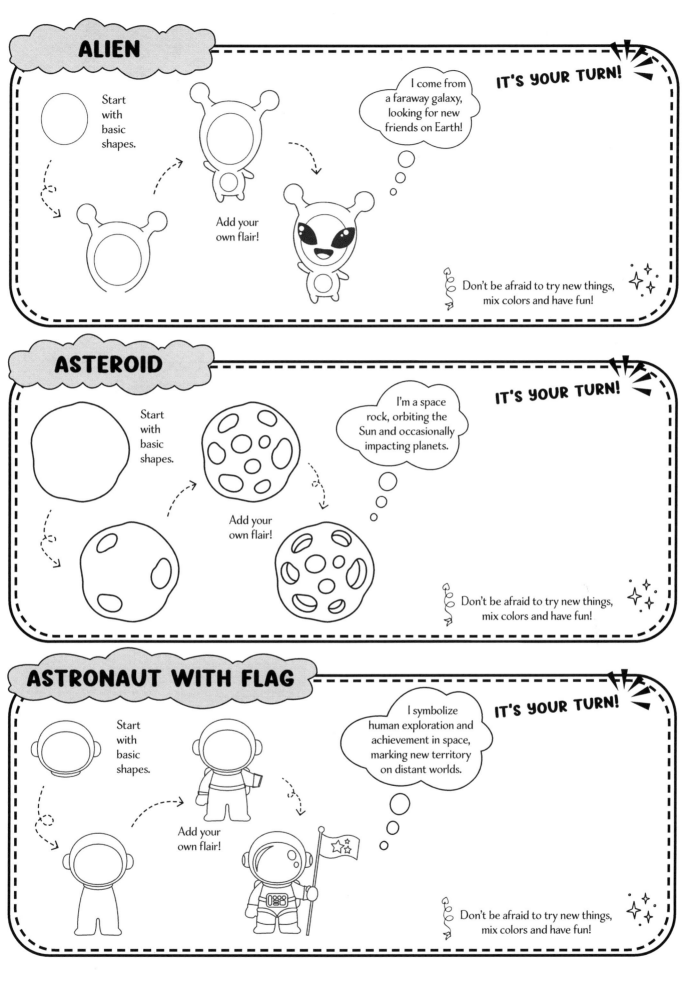

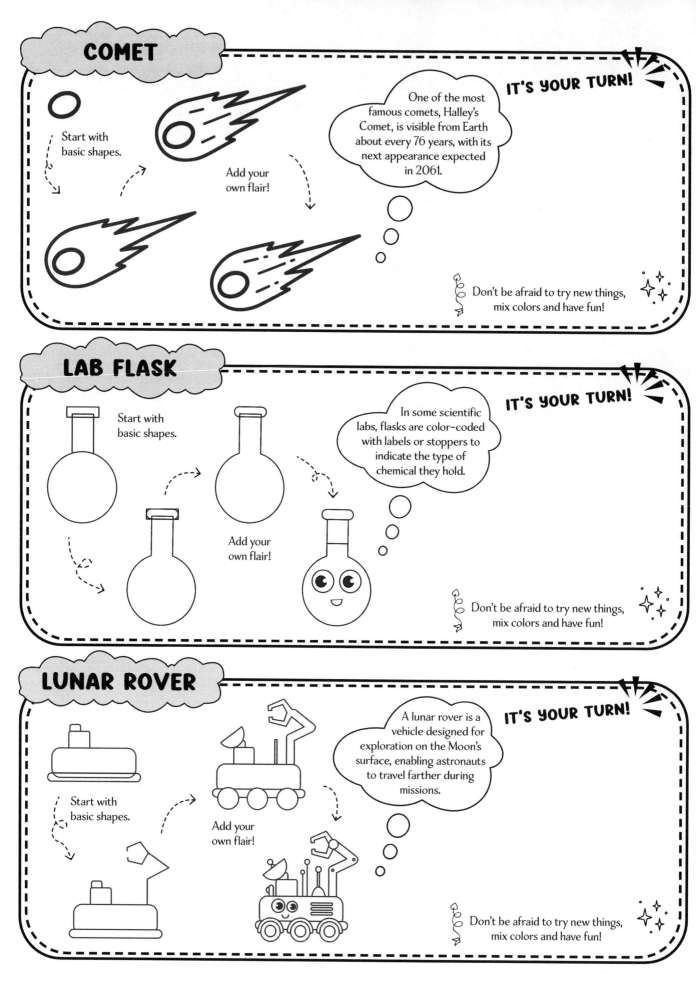

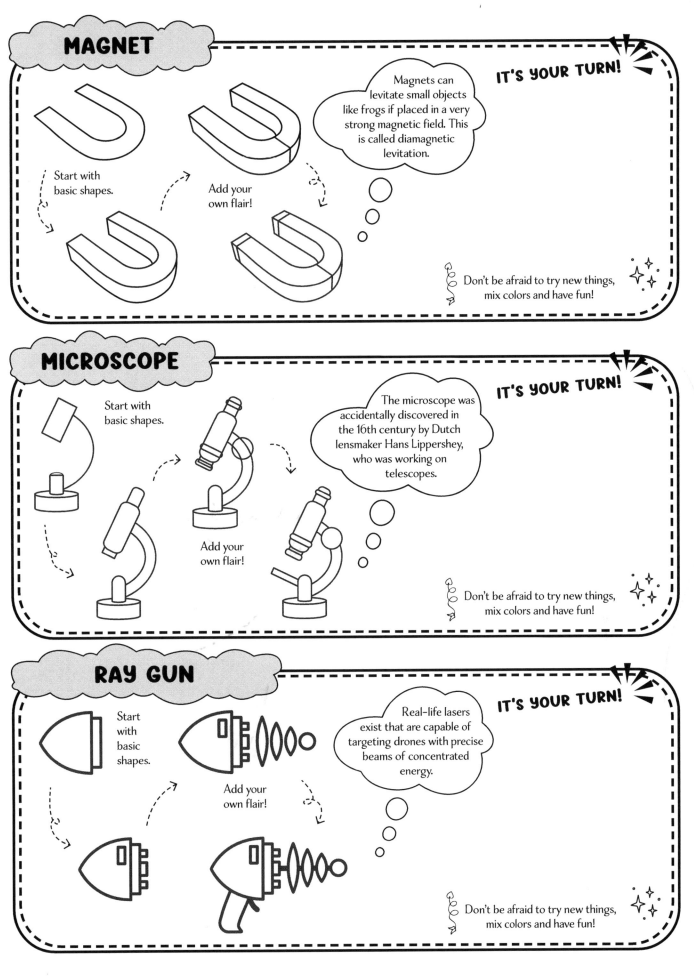

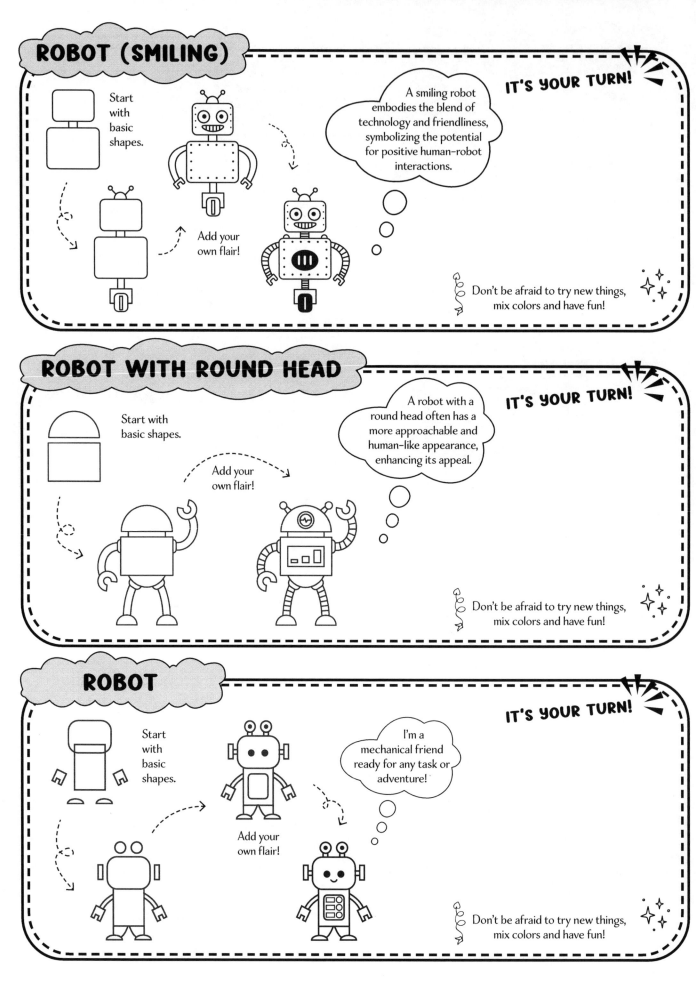

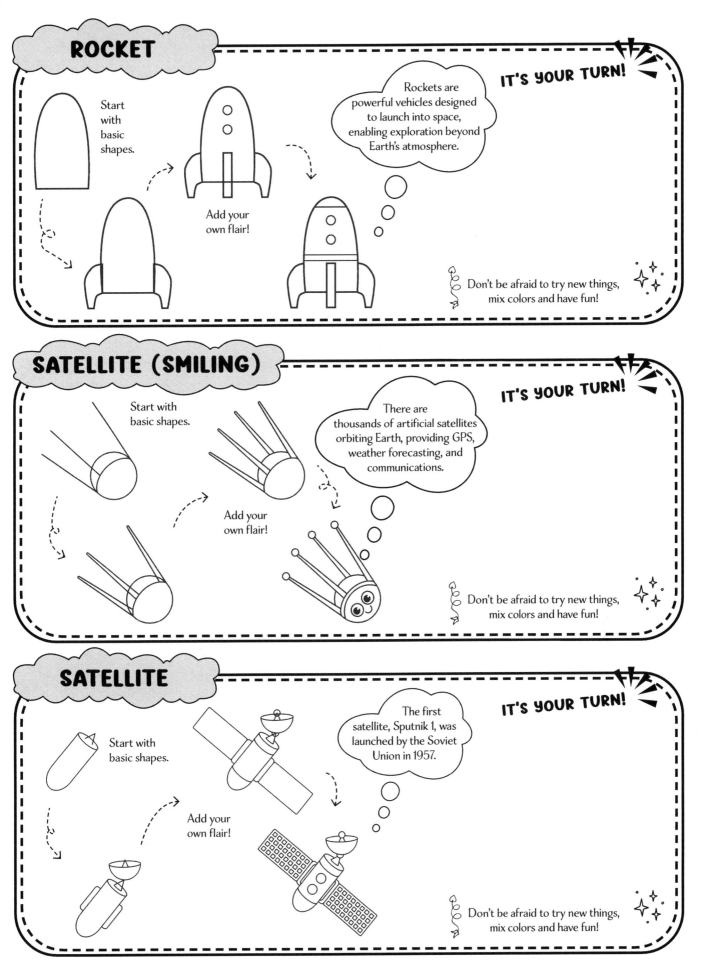

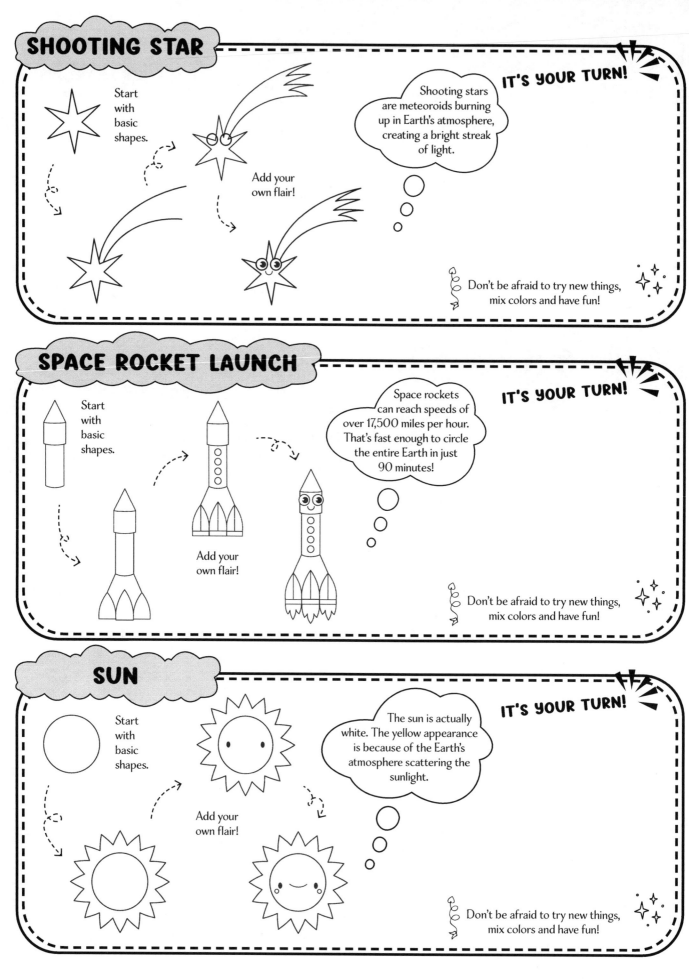

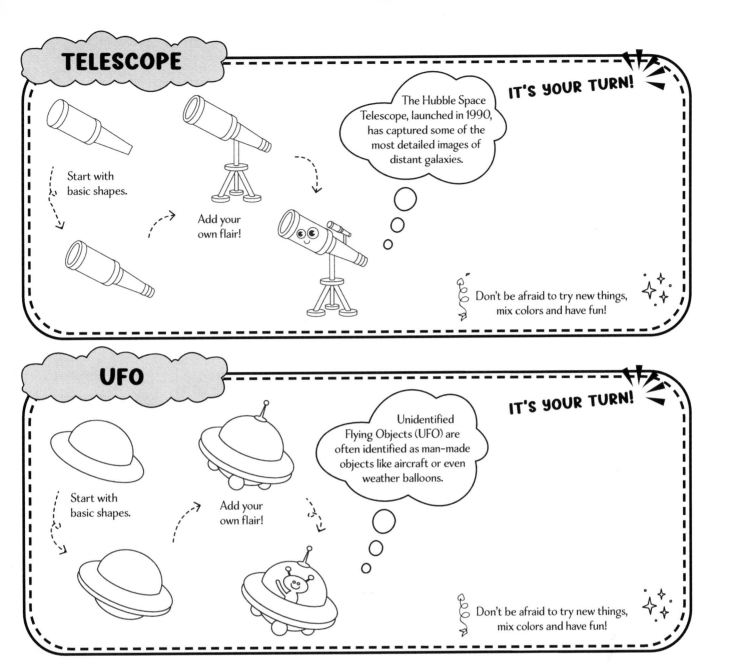

Sports, Fast Food and Everyday Things

Bring us to life with your colors!

It's time to draw some things you see almost every day! Like some **slippers**, a **watch**, and even your **bed**. Once you've learned to draw these everyday things, you can draw almost everything in your **room**!

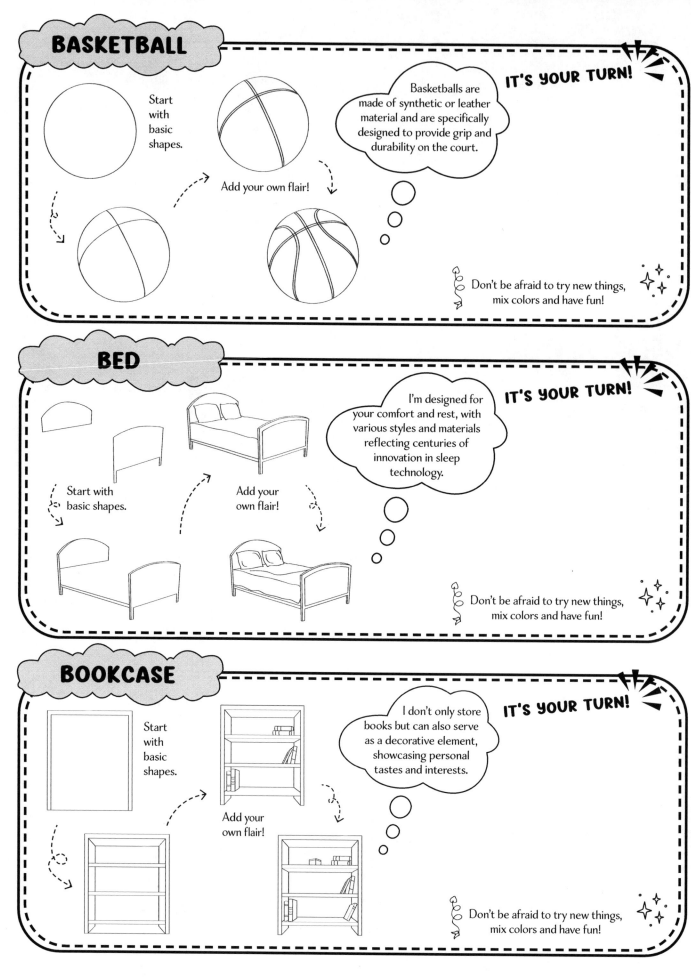

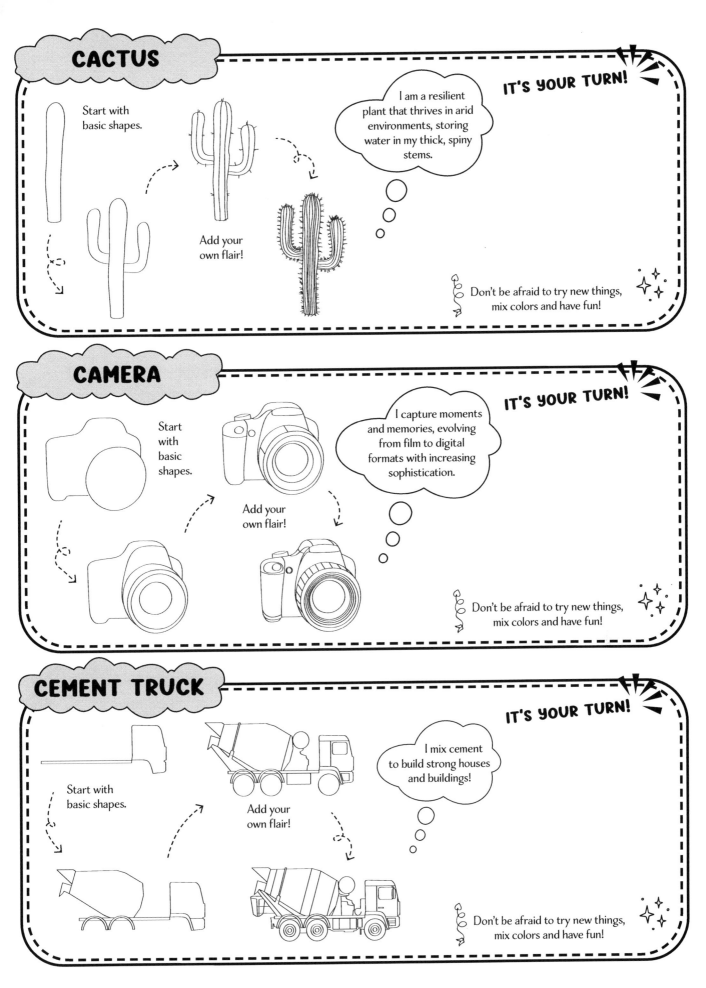

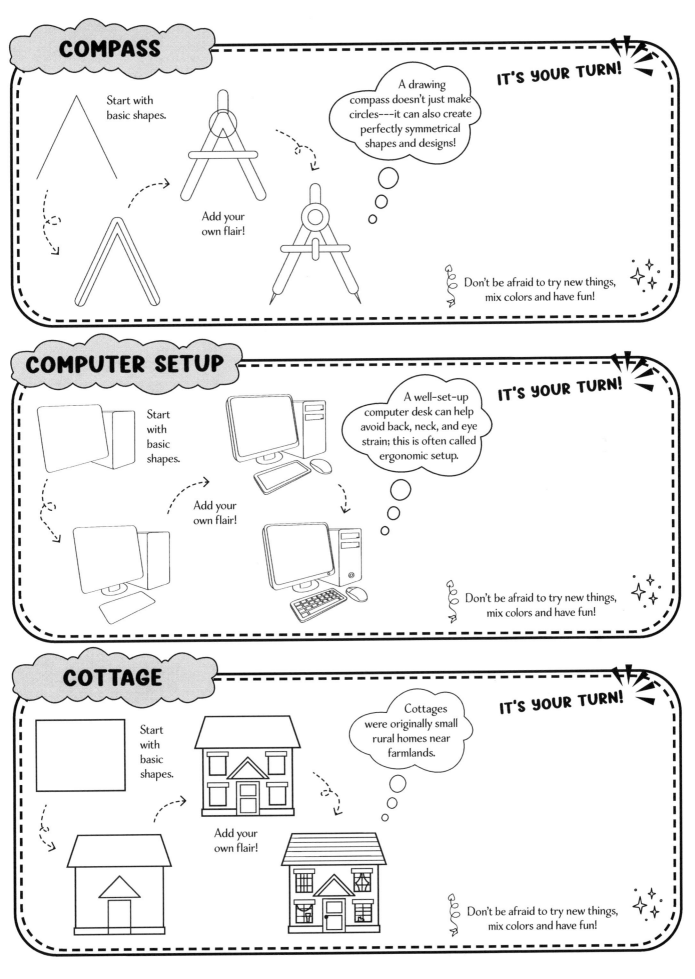

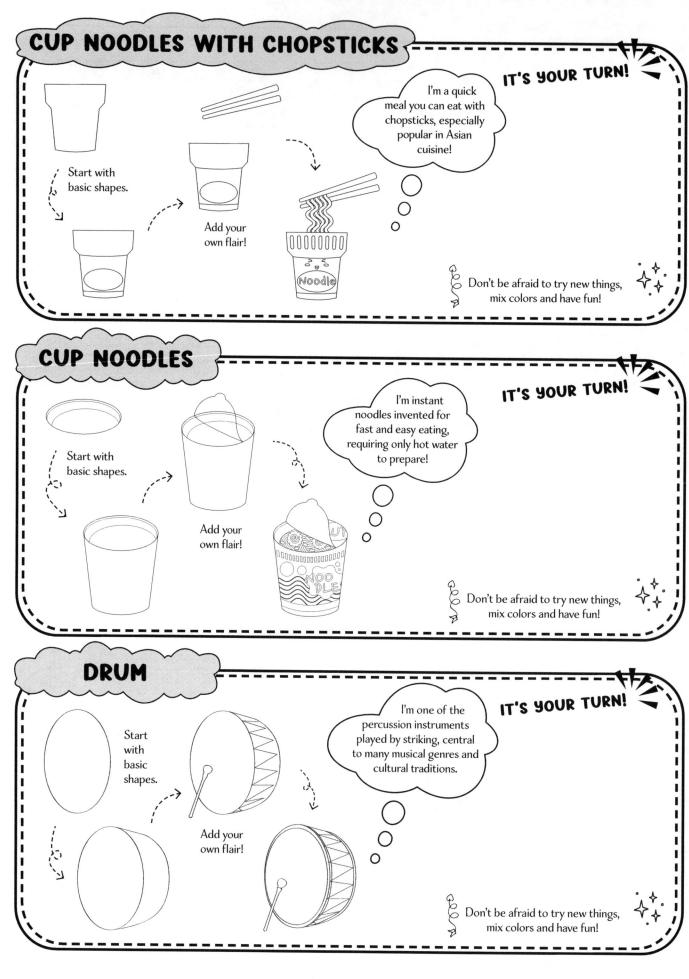

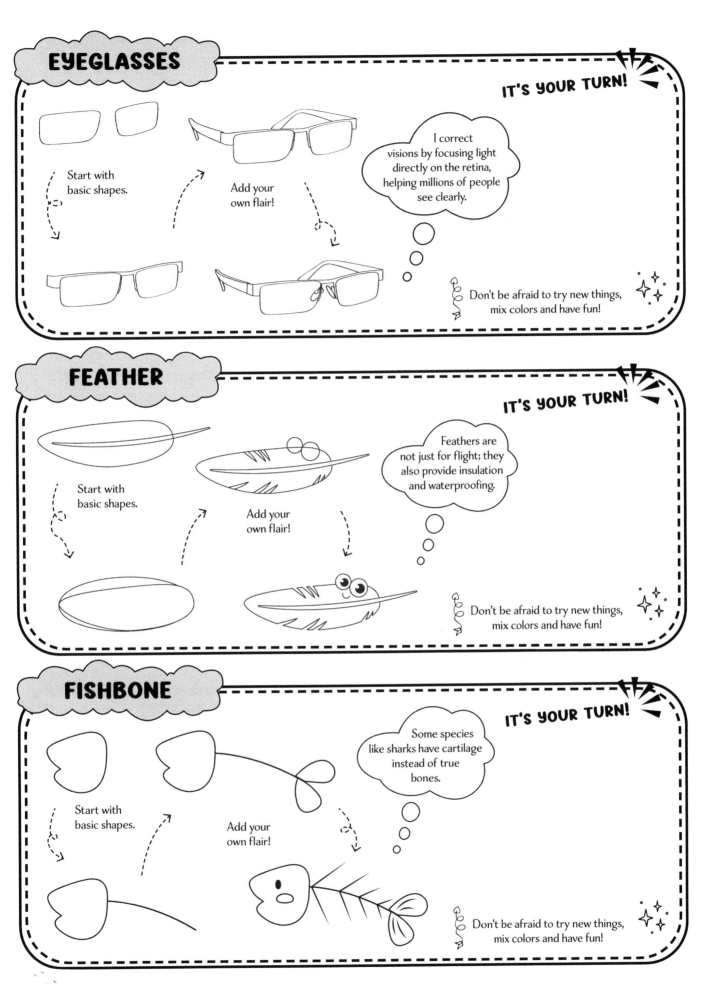

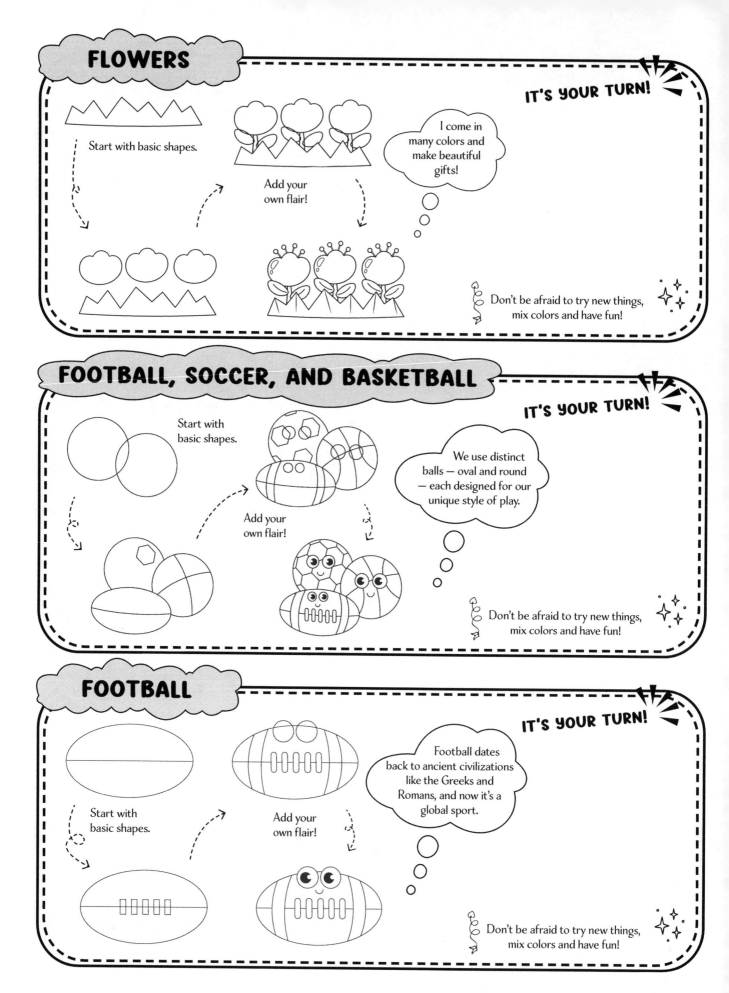

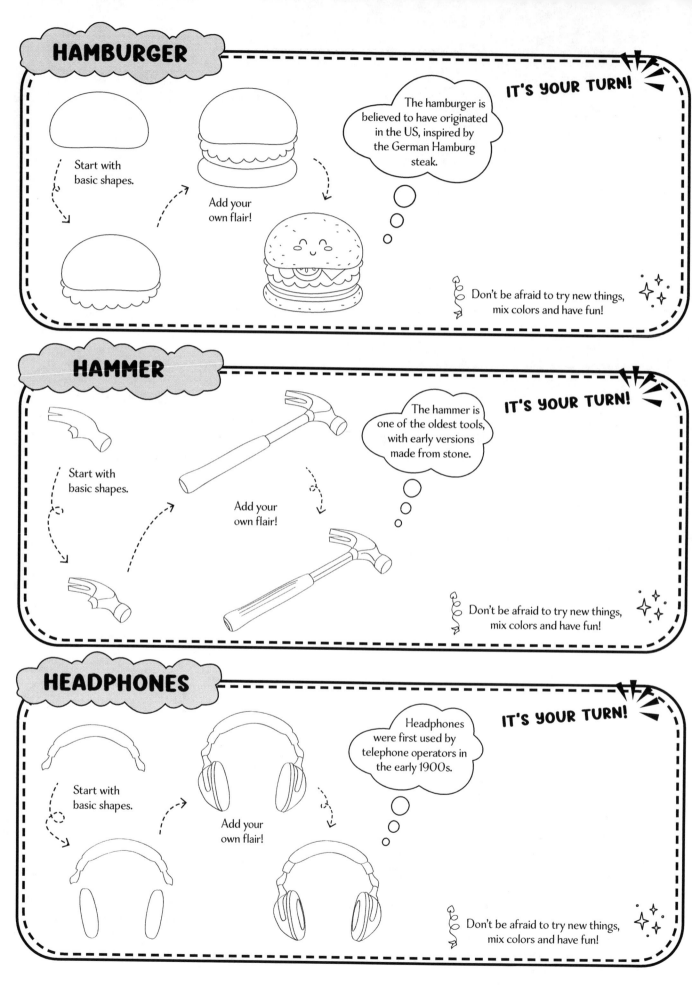

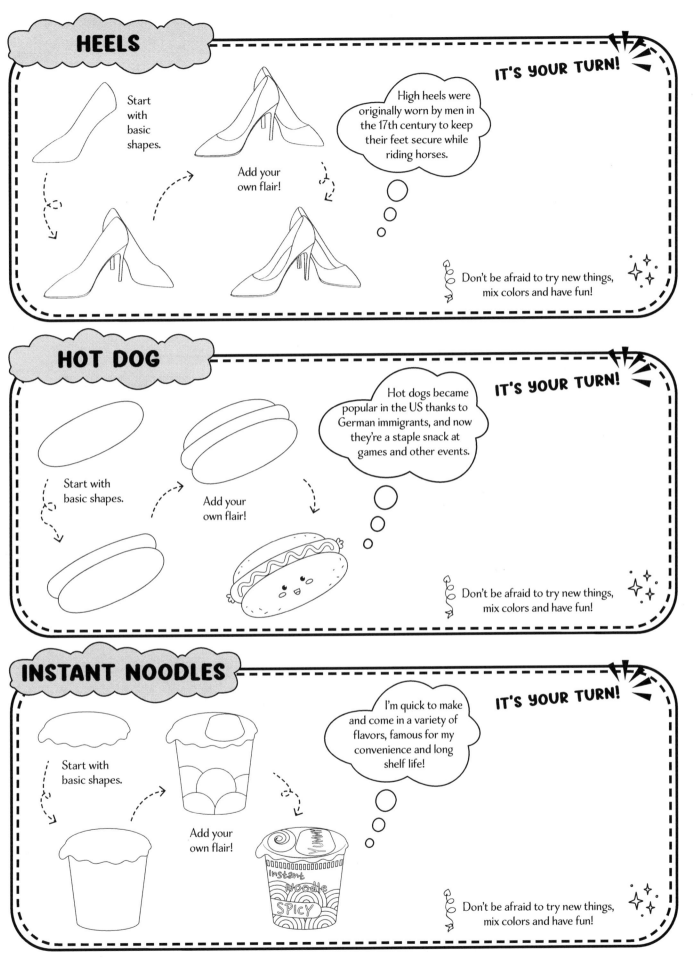

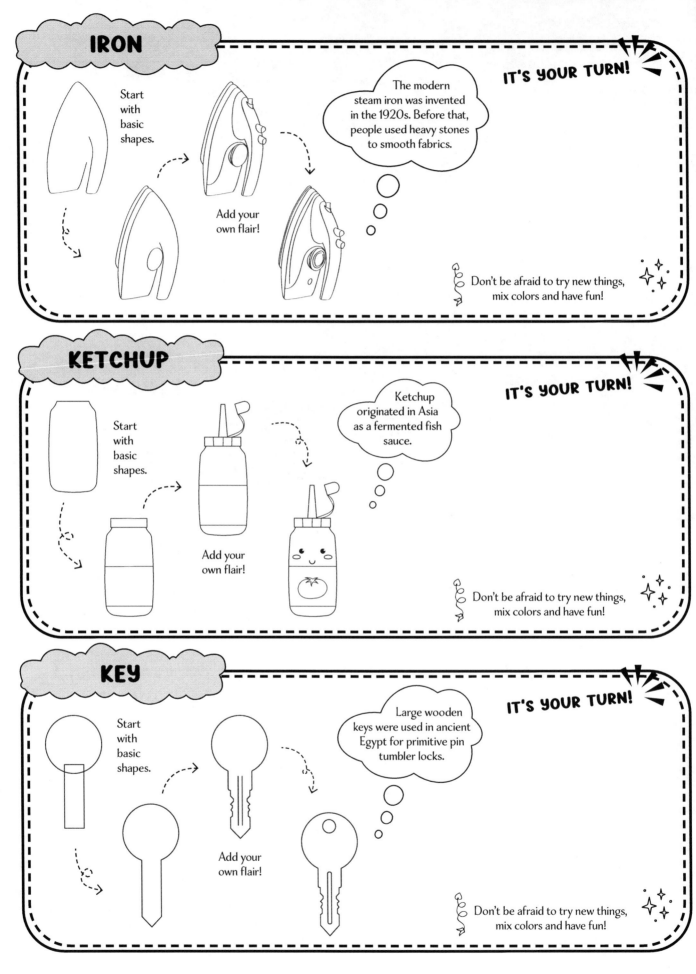

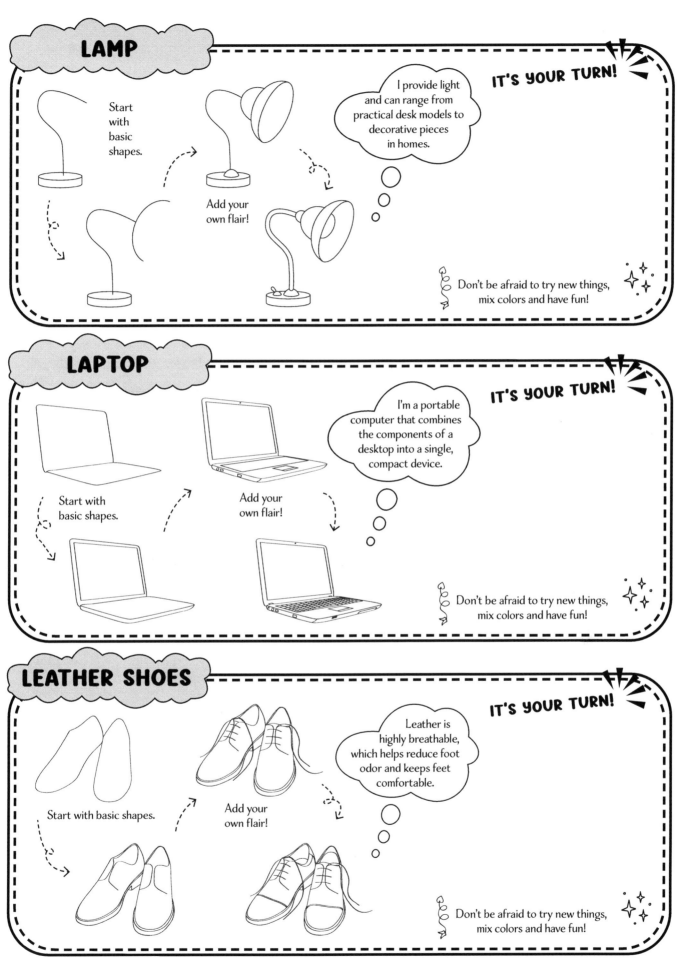

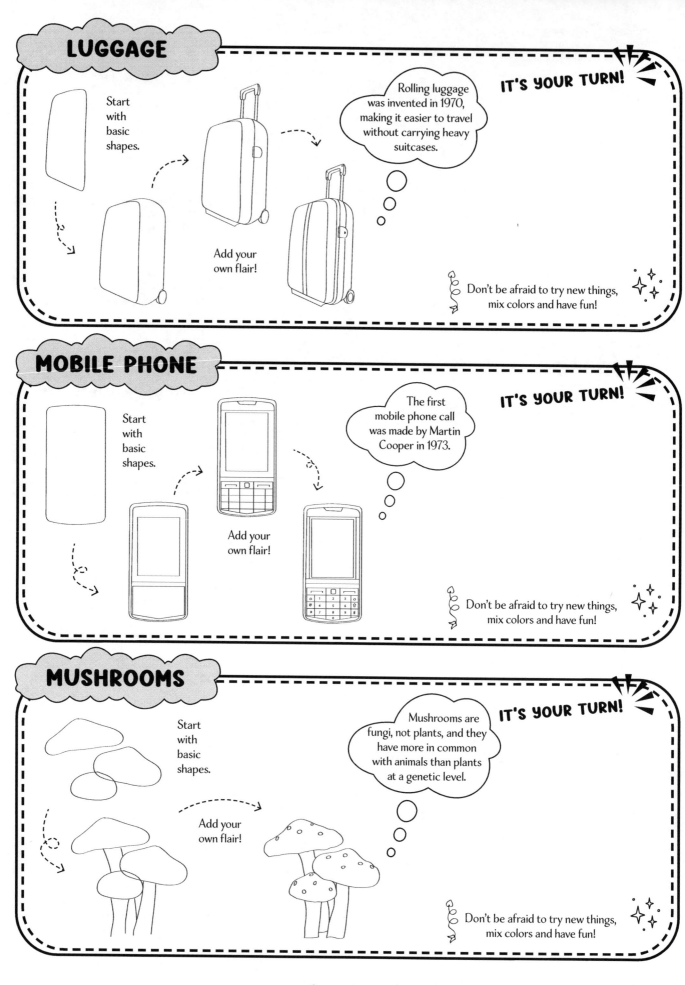

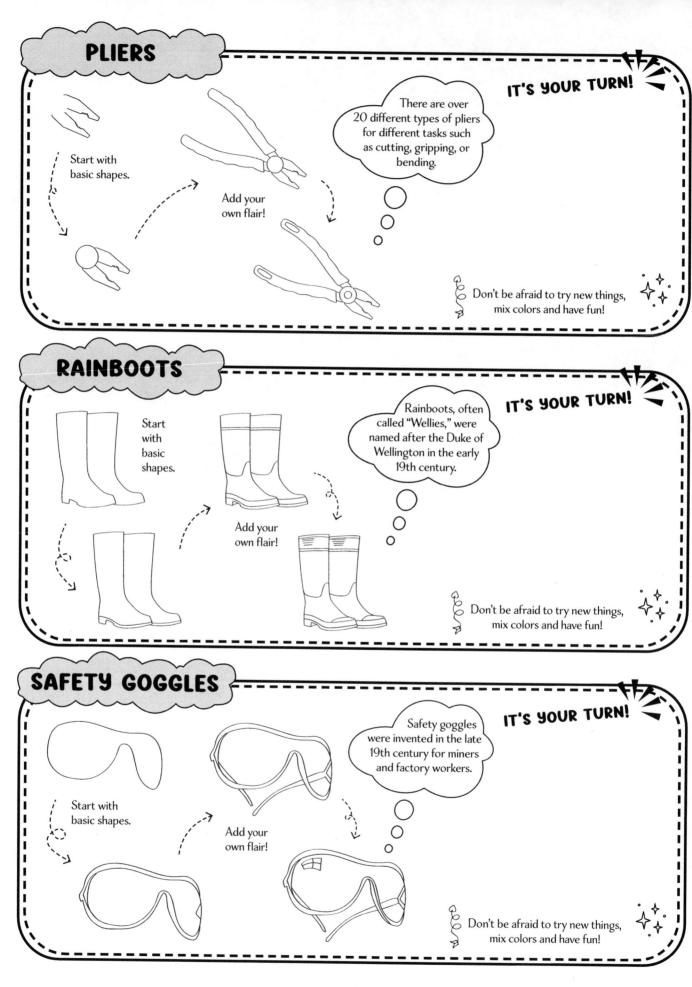

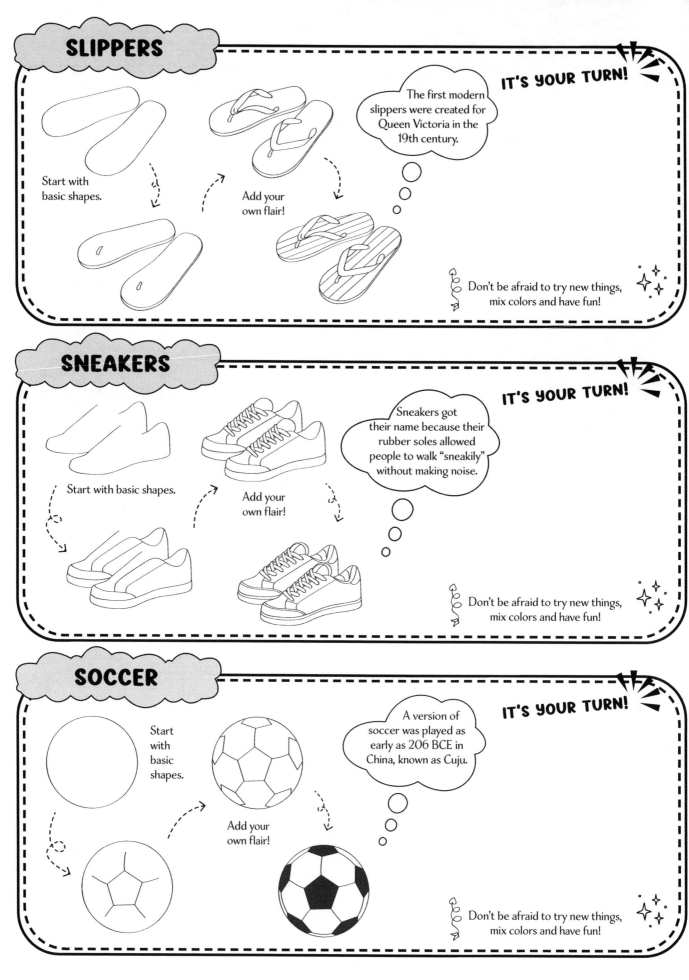

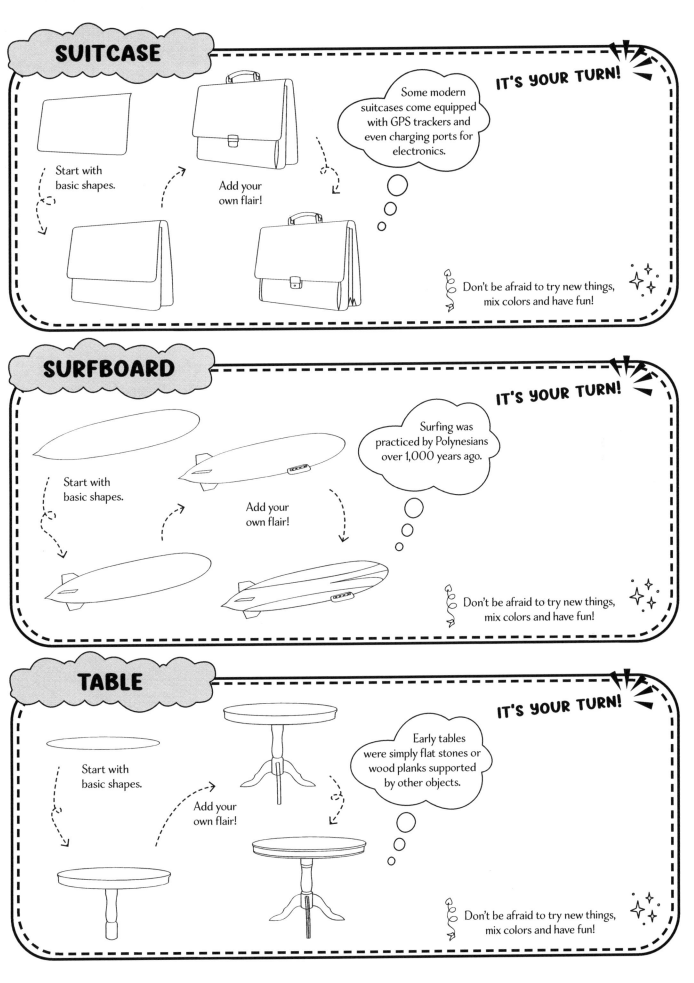

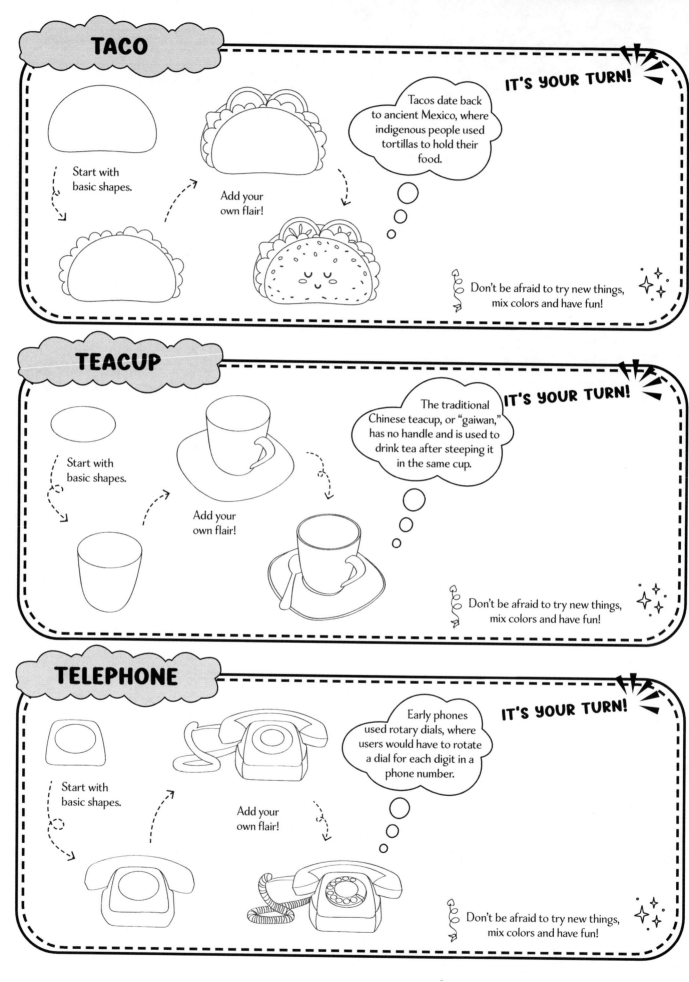

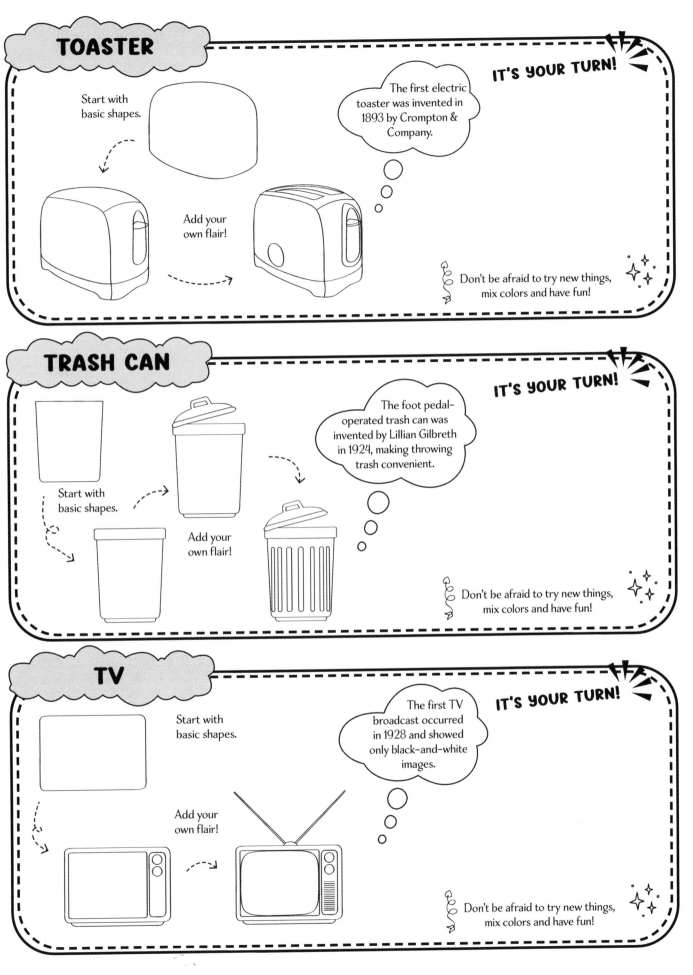

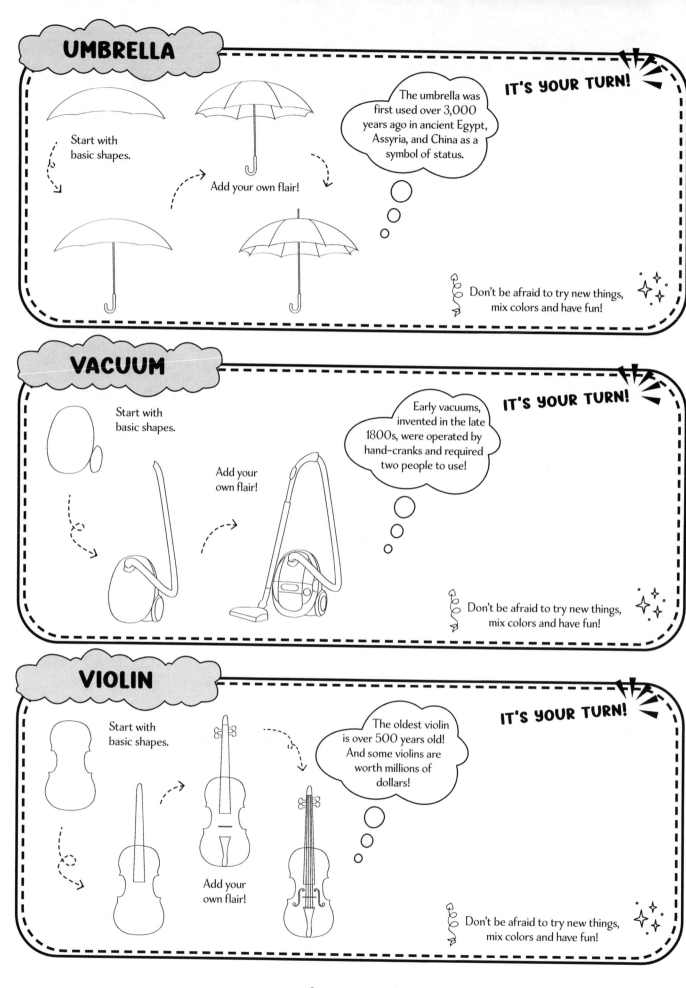

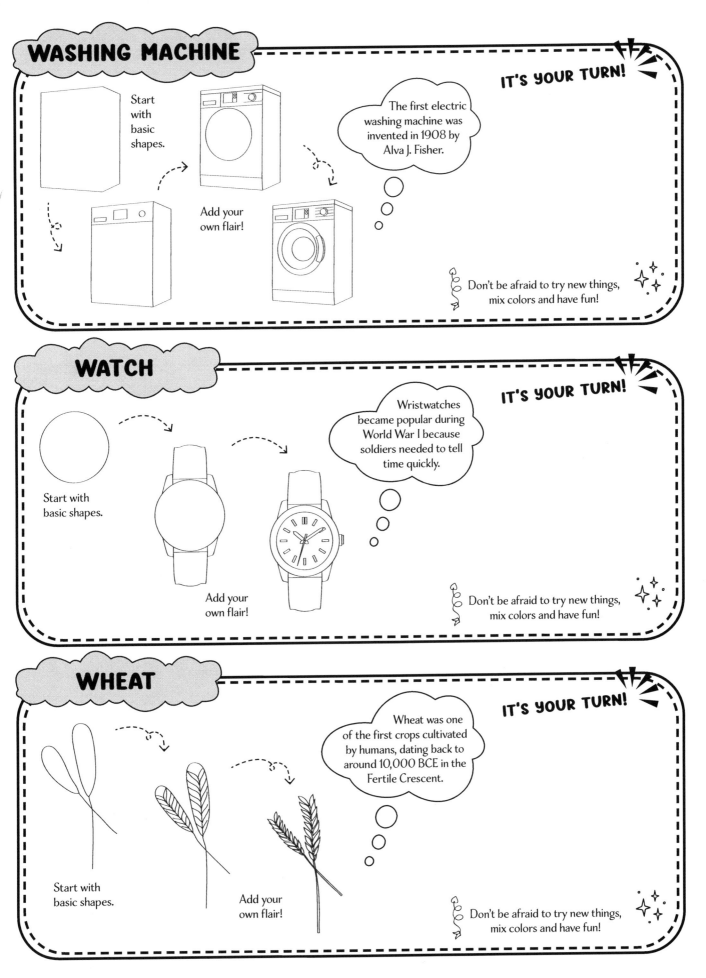

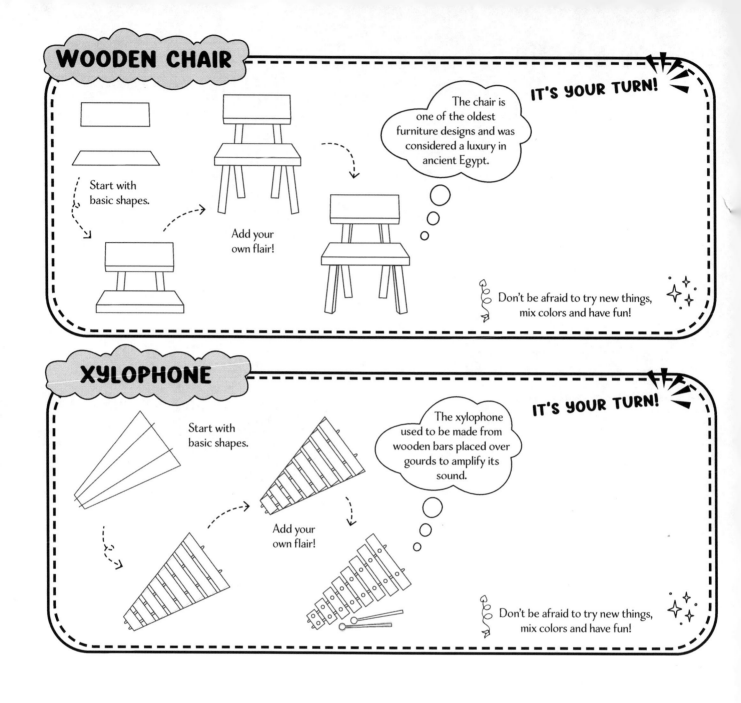

YOU ARE AWESOME!

Awesome job drawing all those cool things! Now you can sketch in your notebooks, make awesome greeting cards, and even create posters to hang on your wall.

You can also surprise your friends and family with your drawings as gifts! There's so much you can do with your new skills.

What's next on your drawing list? Keep practicing and become a drawing master. Don't forget to check out our other how-to-draw books for more epic ideas!

Keep drawing and have fun!

Made in the USA
Columbia, SC
12 July 2025